HOUSING ISSUES, LAWS AND PROGRAMS

NO ONE HOME

CHALLENGES AND COSTS OF VACANT PROPERTIES

HOUSING ISSUES, LAWS AND PROGRAMS

Additional books in this series can be found on Nova's website under the Series tab.

Additional E-books in this series can be found on Nova's website under the E-books tab.

SOCIAL ISSUES, JUSTICE AND STATUS

Additional books in this series can be found on Nova's website under the Series tab.

Additional E-books in this series can be found on Nova's website under the E-books tab.

HOUSING ISSUES, LAWS AND PROGRAMS

NO ONE HOME

CHALLENGES AND COSTS OF VACANT PROPERTIES

MILTON L. JACKSON
AND
GENE A. WHITE
EDITORS

Nova Science Publishers, Inc.
New York

For permission to use material from this book please contact us:
Telephone 631-231-7269; Fax 631-231-8175
Web Site: http://www.novapublishers.com

LIBRARY OF CONGRESS CATALOGING-IN-PUBLICATION DATA

ISBN: 978-1-61942-829-4

Published by Nova Science Publishers, Inc. † New York

CONTENTS

PREFACE

During the continuing foreclosure crisis and economic downturn, increased numbers of vacant residential properties are becoming vandalized or dilapidated, attracting crime, and contributing to neighborhood decline in many communities across the country. Even though homeowners whose properties are being foreclosed upon may continue to occupy their properties until after a foreclosure sale occurs, many leave their homes during the foreclosure process. In addition, properties for which a new entity has assumed ownership through foreclosure may be vacant until the property is resold. This book explores the concern over the costs that foreclosed and unattended vacant homes are creating for local communities and the strategies state and local governments are using to address unattended vacant property problems and the challenges those governments face.

Chapter 1 - Vacant and unattended residential properties can attract crime, cause blight, and pose a threat to public safety. While homeowners or mortgage owners—including the mortgage servicers that administer loans on behalf of loan owners—are responsible for maintaining vacant properties with mortgages undergoing foreclosure, the costs local governments incur to mitigate any unsafe conditions can be significant. GAO was asked to examine (1) trends in the number of vacant properties and how they relate to the recent increase in foreclosures, (2) the types of costs that vacant properties create and who bears the responsibility for these properties and their costs, and (3) state and local government strategies to address vacant properties and the federal role in assisting these efforts. GAO analyzed Census Bureau vacancy data and data on property maintenance costs from the Federal Housing Administration (FHA) and two housing-related government-sponsored enterprises (GSE). GAO conducted case studies in nine cities selected to provide a range of local economic and housing conditions, rates of foreclosure, and geographic locations. GAO also interviewed local officials, representatives of community development organizations, federal agencies, and mortgage servicers, among others.

Chapter 2 - Good morning. I very much appreciate your invitation to speak today. The theme of this ninth annual Federal Reserve Bank of Cleveland Policy Summit, “Housing, Human Capital, and Inequality,” could not be timelier. Almost no community in America has escaped the effects of the economic downturn, but many low- and moderate-income communities were hit especially hard, including a large number in and around our host city of Cleveland. As one sobering example, almost 10 percent of current Cleveland residents who have ever taken out a mortgage have a foreclosure reflected on their credit report--a rate double that of the rest of the nation. I will focus today on the state of the housing market and emphasize developments pertaining to low- and moderate-income neighborhoods. I will then discuss policy initiatives to address some of the challenges confronting the housing market.

Chapter 3 - Good afternoon. I’d like to join my colleagues in welcoming you to the Federal Reserve Board. This policy forum, “The Housing Market Going Forward: Lessons Learned from the Recent Crisis,” has been designed to connect lessons learned from the recent past with policy alternatives that may affect the market for years to come. Determining the key lessons and getting this connection right are important, and as you have already heard, perhaps not as easy as it might sound. I would like to offer some suggestions that I think could help. Before I begin, though, I should clarify that the ideas I will be discussing do not necessarily reflect the opinions of my colleagues on the Federal Reserve Board and that these suggestions should not be construed as policy of the Board or the Federal Open Market Committee.

In: No One Home ISBN: 978-1-61942-829-4
Editors: M. L. Jackson and G. A. White

Chapter 1

VACANT PROPERTIES: GROWING NUMBER INCREASES COMMUNITIES' COSTS AND CHALLENGES*

United States Government Accountability Office

WHY GAO DID THIS STUDY

Vacant and unattended residential properties can attract crime, cause blight, and pose a threat to public safety. While homeowners or mortgage owners—including the mortgage servicers that administer loans on behalf of loan owners—are responsible for maintaining vacant properties with mortgages undergoing foreclosure, the costs local governments incur to mitigate any unsafe conditions can be significant.

GAO was asked to examine (1) trends in the number of vacant properties and how they relate to the recent increase in foreclosures, (2) the types of costs that vacant properties create and who bears the responsibility for these properties and their costs, and (3) state and local government strategies to address vacant properties and the federal role in assisting these efforts. GAO analyzed Census Bureau vacancy data and data on property maintenance costs

---

* This is an edited, reformatted and augmented version of the United States Government Accountability Office publication Report to the Ranking Member, Subcommittee on Regulatory Affairs, Stimulus Oversight, and Government Spending, Committee on Oversight and Government Reform, House of Representatives GAO-12-34, dated November 2011.

from the Federal Housing Administration (FHA) and two housing-related government-sponsored enterprises (GSE). GAO conducted case studies in nine cities selected to provide a range of local economic and housing conditions, rates of foreclosure, and geographic locations. GAO also interviewed local officials, representatives of community development organizations, federal agencies, and mortgage servicers, among others.

The Federal Reserve, Census, Office of Comptroller of the Currency, FHA, Federal Housing Finance Agency, and GSEs provided technical comments, which GAO incorporated as appropriate. Treasury commented that the report was informative and noted the need for all stakeholders to analyze policy responses to this issue.

WHAT GAO FOUND

According to Census Bureau data, nonseasonal vacant properties have increased 51 percent nationally from nearly 7 million in 2000 to 10 million in April 2010, with 10 states seeing increases of 70 percent or more. High foreclosure rates have contributed to the additional vacancies. Population declines in certain cities and high unemployment also may have contributed to increased vacancies. However, these data do not indicate the number of vacant properties that are inadequately maintained and imposing costs on local governments.

If a homeowner abandons a property, servicers may have the right under typical mortgage agreements to conduct certain maintenance, although they generally are not obligated to do so until they assume ownership on behalf of the loan owner after foreclosure. In 2010, the GSEs reimbursed servicers or vendors over $953 million for property maintenance costs. However, local governments reported spending millions of dollars—including federal funds—on vacant properties that are not adequately maintained. For example, Detroit spent about $20 million since May 2009 to demolish almost 4,000 vacant properties. Unattended vacant properties produce public safety costs and lower communities' tax revenues due to the decline in value of surrounding properties, with some studies finding that vacant foreclosed properties may have reduced prices of nearby homes by $8,600 to $17,000 per property in specific cities.

Cities and states are implementing a variety of strategies to minimize the negative impacts of vacant properties but face various challenges. For example, some local governments are creating special entities called land banks that acquire and hold vacant properties for later development, sale, or demolition. However, difficulty obtaining adequate and sustained funding and finding buyers for the properties can hamper these local efforts. Some cities have passed ordinances that require servicers to notify the city when a property they are managing becomes vacant and attempt to hold them responsible for maintenance.

However, localities often lack resources or staff to enforce these requirements fully. Some suggest fewer properties would become vacant if servicers had to account for communities' costs—such as for policing and fires— when considering whether to modify loans or foreclose, but servicers and others questioned the feasibility and effectiveness of such an approach. Local officials and community groups said they need more funds and increased oversight by federal regulators to ensure that servicers comply with local property maintenance codes.

ABBREVIATIONS

ACS	American Community Survey
CDBG	Community Development Block Grant
CDC	community development corporation
FDIC	Federal Deposit Insurance Corporation
FHA	Federal Housing Administration
FHFA	Federal Housing Finance Agency
GSE	government-sponsored enterprise
HAMP	Home Affordable Modification Program
HUD	Department of Housing and Urban Development
NEO CANDO	Northeast Ohio Community and Neighborhood Data for Organizing
NPV	net present value
NSP	Neighborhood Stabilization Program
OCC	Office of the Comptroller of the Currency
REO	real-estate owned
USPS	U.S. Postal Service

November 4, 2011

The Honorable Dennis J. Kucinich
Ranking Member
Subcommittee on Regulatory Affairs,
Stimulus Oversight, and Government Spending Committee on Oversight and Government Reform House of Representatives

Dear Mr. Kucinich,

During the continuing foreclosure crisis and economic downturn, increased numbers of vacant residential properties are becoming vandalized or dilapidated, attracting crime, and contributing to neighborhood decline in many communities across the country. Even though homeowners whose properties are being foreclosed upon may continue to occupy their properties until after a foreclosure sale occurs, many leave their homes during the foreclosure process. In addition, properties for which a new entity has assumed ownership through foreclosure may be vacant until the property is resold. If neither of these owners nor the mortgage servicer—the entity that manages mortgage loans and foreclosures on behalf of banks and other holders of mortgage loans—acts to maintain these vacant homes, these properties can deteriorate, increasing blight in the community. Unattended vacant properties can also increase costs for local governments that must expend resources to inspect the properties and mitigate any unsafe conditions, including demolishing some properties.[1]

Because of the impact of housing on the national and local economies, the federal government has attempted to address issues arising from the financial crisis that began in 2007 and its aftermath. As part of the Troubled Asset Relief Program created to restore stability and liquidity to the financial system, Congress called for the Department of the Treasury (Treasury) to preserve homeownership and protect home values.[2] In addition, Congress created the Neighborhood Stabilization Program (NSP), which provides grants to states and local governments to help reduce the number of foreclosed and abandoned properties and restore depressed local housing markets.[3]

Your letter expressed concern over the costs that foreclosed and unattended vacant homes are creating for local communities and asked us to review the strategies state and local governments are using to address unattended vacant property problems and the challenges those governments face. Specifically, this report addresses (1) trends in the number of vacant properties and how they relate to the recent increase in foreclosures, (2) the types of costs that vacant properties create and who bears the responsibility for these properties and their costs, and (3) state and local government strategies for addressing vacant properties and the federal role in assisting these efforts.

To address these objectives, we analyzed data on vacant residential housing units from the Census Bureau (Census) from 2000 to 2010, as well as from the U.S. Postal Service (USPS) as of the second quarter of 2010. We also analyzed data on property maintenance costs from two housing-related government-sponsored enterprises (GSE)—Fannie Mae and Freddie Mac—and the Department of Housing and Urban Development's Federal Housing Administration (FHA). We assessed the reliability of the data we used by reviewing past GAO and other assessments of the data and interviewing knowledgeable agency officials. We determined that these data were sufficiently reliable for use in the report. We also collected information about local strategies by reviewing literature and conducting case studies in nine localities that we selected based on high vacancy and foreclosure rates, geographic location, economic conditions, and foreclosure processes. These localities were Baltimore, Maryland; Cape Coral, Florida; Chicago, Illinois; Cleveland, Ohio; Detroit, Michigan; Indianapolis, Indiana; Indio, California; Las Vegas, Nevada; and Tucson, Arizona. In each location, we interviewed local government officials and representatives of nonprofit and community development organizations. In addition, we interviewed code enforcement officials in two states that recently passed laws pertaining to maintenance of vacant properties in foreclosure—New York and New Jersey. We also interviewed staff from one of the largest maintenance companies that conducts property inspections and maintenance on behalf of services nationwide, academic researchers, GSE staff, and five mortgage servicers—including some of the largest firms and those that specialized in subprime loans. In addition, we interviewed representatives of federal agencies, including the Board of Governors of the Federal Reserve System (Federal Reserve), Census, Federal Deposit Insurance Corporation (FDIC), Office of the Comptroller of the Currency (OCC), Department of Housing and Urban Development (HUD), Federal Housing Finance Agency (FHFA), and Treasury. Appendix I contains more information about our objectives, scope, and methodology.

We conducted this performance audit from November 2010 to November 2011 in accordance with generally accepted government auditing standards. Those standards require that we plan and perform the audit to obtain sufficient, appropriate evidence to provide a reasonable basis for our findings and conclusions based on our audit objectives. We believe that the evidence obtained provides a reasonable basis for our findings and conclusions based on our audit objectives.

BACKGROUND

Multiple entities have specific roles regarding mortgage loans and the maintenance of properties that experience foreclosure. When individuals purchase residential real property with borrowed funds, they usually enter into a contractual agreement, typically called a promissory note, in which they agree, among other things, to make principal and interest payments to the originating lender for a period of time and to maintain the property in order to prevent it from deteriorating or decreasing in value due to its condition. Borrowers usually also sign a mortgage or deed of trust that pledges the underlying property as collateral against the borrower's default. The holders of these documents are allowed to record a lien against the property and are granted the right to seize, and usually sell, the property should the borrower fail to pay.[4]

Institutions that originate home mortgage loans generally do not hold all such loans as assets on their balance sheets but instead sell them to other financial institutions or the GSEs, Fannie Mae or Freddie Mac, for the purpose of securitizing them.[5] Through securitization, the purchasers of these mortgages package them into pools and issue securities known as mortgage-backed securities for which the mortgage loans serve as collateral. In some cases, loans are purchased by financial institutions and issued as mortgage-backed securities to investors without any involvement of the GSEs or FHA in securitizations known as "private label." In other cases, mortgage-backed securities are backed by pools of GSE loans or mortgage loans insured by federal agencies, such as FHA.[6] Mortgage-backed securities pay interest and principal to their investors, which include other financial institutions, pension funds, or other institutional investors. The GSEs guarantee investors in their securities the timely payment of principal and interest. The Government National Mortgage Association (Ginnie Mae), a wholly owned government corporation, guarantees the timely payment of principal and interest on securities backed by federally insured or guaranteed loans.

After a mortgage originator sells its loans to an investor or to an institution that will securitize them, another financial institution or other entity is appointed as the servicer to manage payment collections and other activities associated with these loans. Mortgage servicers, which can be large mortgage finance companies, commercial banks, or small specialty companies unaffiliated with a larger financial institution, earn a fee for acting as the servicer on behalf of the purchaser of the loans. Servicing duties can involve sending borrowers monthly account statements, answering customer-service inquiries, collecting monthly mortgage payments, maintaining escrow accounts for property taxes and hazard insurance, and forwarding proper payments to the mortgage owners. In the event that a borrower becomes delinquent on loan payments, servicers also initiate and conduct foreclosures in order to obtain the proceeds from the sale of the property on behalf of the owners of the loans. Servicers often contract with third-party vendors to conduct some of their responsibilities. For example, they may hire property maintenance companies to inspect and conduct maintenance on properties. The duties of servicers may vary based on the entity on whose behalf they are servicing the loans. For the loans they have purchased, Fannie Mae and Freddie Mac each have issued servicing guidelines that must be followed by entities servicing loans on their behalf. In addition, FHA has specific servicer guidelines for entities servicing FHA-insured loans. For loans that are in private-label securities, servicers' duties are specified in a contract called a pooling and servicing agreement, which may place similar expectations on these servicers as the Fannie Mae or Freddie Mac standards.

If a borrower defaults on a mortgage loan secured by the home, the mortgage holder is entitled to pursue foreclosure. Once the borrower is in default, the servicer must decide whether to pursue a home retention workout or foreclosure alternative, such as a short sale, or initiate foreclosure.[7] If the servicer determines that foreclosure is the most appropriate option, it follows one of two foreclosure methods, depending on state law. In a judicial foreclosure, a judge presides over the process in a court proceeding. Servicers initiate a formal foreclosure action by filing a lawsuit with a court. A non-judicial foreclosure process takes place outside the courtroom, and is typically conducted by the trustee named in the deed of trust document. Trustees, and sometimes servicers, generally send a notice of default to the borrower and publish a notice of sale in area newspapers or legal publications.

At a foreclosure sale or auction, if no third party has the winning bid, the servicer can obtain title to the property on behalf of the mortgage owner and sell it to repay the loan. Servicers transfer foreclosed properties, referred to as real-estate owned (REO) properties, from loans that were owned by the GSEs or insured by FHA to those entities within designated time periods following the foreclosure sale. The GSEs and FHA have contractors and other entities that manage the properties on their behalf during the postforeclosure period. Unless servicing agreements for loans in securitization trusts require the properties to be transferred to another party, servicers generally hold the remaining REO properties in their inventory and manage them until they are resold. Several states have enacted "redemption" laws that give borrowers the opportunity to match the winning bids from the foreclosure sale and reclaim their properties. After foreclosure sales and applicable redemption periods, servicers or entities working on behalf of the GSEs and FHA typically proceed with eviction proceedings if foreclosed properties are not already vacant and then market and sell the properties.[8]

Federal Agencies Involved in Overseeing Mortgage Servicers and Funding Housing Programs

Several federal agencies share responsibility for regulating the banking industry in relation to the origination and servicing of mortgage loans.[9] Various agencies oversee federally and state-chartered banks and their mortgage-related subsidiaries depending on which agency granted the institution's operating charter. At the federal level, OCC has authority to oversee nationally chartered banks and federally chartered savings associations, or thrifts, (including mortgage operating subsidiaries). The Federal Reserve oversees insured state-chartered banks that are members of the Federal Reserve, as well as holding companies for thrifts and any lenders owned by these companies. The Federal Reserve also has general authority over bank holding companies, including having responsibility for oversight of any nonbank subsidiaries of these companies that conduct mortgage servicing activities. FDIC oversees insured state-chartered banks that are not members of the Federal Reserve System and state-chartered thrifts. Both the Federal Reserve and FDIC share oversight with the state regulatory authority that chartered the bank. In addition, the Bureau of Consumer Financial Protection has the authority to supervise mortgage servicers with respect to federal consumer financial law.[10]

Other agencies also are involved in overseeing certain aspects of U.S. mortgage markets but do not have supervisory authority over mortgage servicers. For example, FHFA has direct supervisory authority over Fannie Mae's and Freddie Mac's activities but does not have supervisory authority over servicers in general. The FHA oversees institutions approved to service loans that FHA insures for the servicers' compliance with servicing regulations on, for example, the timing of foreclosure initiation. Similarly, Treasury has a contractual relationship with servicers that voluntarily participate in the Home Affordable Modification Program (HAMP), which is a program designed to help borrowers avoid foreclosure and stay in their homes by providing incentives for servicers to perform loan modifications. To oversee compliance with this program's guidelines, Treasury can conduct reviews of participating servicers.

The federal government also provides funding assistance to state and local governments for various housing-related activities, including for addressing issues related to vacant properties. NSP provides grants to states and local governments both to help reduce the number of foreclosed and abandoned properties and to restore depressed local housing markets. Since 2008, almost $7 billion has been authorized over the course of three phases. In each phase, grantees receiving NSP funds may use them directly or reallocate them to other entities within their states. Grantees must use funds for specifically defined eligible uses to address issues associated with foreclosed and abandoned properties. For example, grantees may choose to acquire and rehabilitate properties for rental or resale or demolish blighted structures. Participants must also follow several key requirements governing the use of NSP funds, such as using the funds in "areas of greatest need" within specified time frames and using a certain percentage of funds to benefit low-income households. Another program administered by HUD, the Community Development Block Grant (CDBG) program, provides grants to localities for 26 eligible activities, including acquisition, administration and planning, economic development, housing, public improvements, and public services, among others. For example, CDBG funds could be used to rehabilitate single-family residential properties.

More Properties Have Become Vacant in Recent Years, in Step with Increased Foreclosures and Unemployment

Various Entities Attempt to Count Vacant Properties but Determining Occupancy Status is Difficult

Some federal agencies compile data on the number of vacant properties in the United States, but using these data to identify unattended vacant properties—that is, properties that are not being maintained and therefore impose costs on the surrounding community—is difficult. The sources of national vacancy data available from federal agencies include two different collection efforts by Census and data that the USPS compiles on vacant addresses.[11] The decennial census is intended to make a complete count of the nation's population and includes questions about housing characteristics such as the total number of occupied and vacant properties. The 2000 and 2010 Census efforts took place over several months beginning in April of each year and recorded the status of vacant properties as of April 1, or Census Day. As part of the 2010 Census, Census mailed questionnaires to more than 120 million housing units and conducted follow-up, door-to-door data collection for almost 47 million households that did not mail back the census forms.[12] A second Census data collection effort that includes information on vacant properties is its American Community Survey (ACS), which it compiles through a survey of 3 million households throughout the year. The ACS data are reported on an annual basis and are also aggregated into 3-year and 5-year datasets. To collect the ACS data, Census mails a questionnaire to a sample of 3 million households and if surveys are not returned, it follows up by telephone if a valid telephone phone number exists. ACS field representatives also conduct door-to-door surveys of a subsample of the households that do not respond to either the mailing or telephone call. Another source of data on the number of vacant properties is compiled by USPS, which maintains a listing of properties that appear to be vacant based on observations by individual postal carriers. The USPS data may not immediately capture a vacant property as USPS does not record a property as vacant until at least 90 days have passed from when vacancy was first suspected.

According to Census and USPS officials, and representatives of one local government, nongovernmental organization, and mortgage servicer, the primary difficulty in accurately determining the total number of vacant properties is identifying whether a property is truly vacant.[13] Methods these entities use generally rely on physical inspection of property exteriors to identify indicators of vacancy, such as broken windows or broken/missing doors, high grass, or uncollected mail. In some cases, Census enumerators or other inspectors may obtain information about the occupancy status of a property from neighbors. Some methods that local government or non-governmental staff also use include reviewing public utility (e.g., water, electricity) usage records as utility shutoffs or very low usage levels can indicate that a property may be vacant. Distinguishing the type of vacant property—for example, whether the property is a vacation home—can also be difficult using exterior inspection methods. Another limitation is that definitions or criteria used to determine vacancy can vary among data collection sources, making comparability of vacancy levels across different sources difficult. In addition, no comprehensive data are available about the duration that properties are vacant. Some properties may be permanently vacant, while others may be reoccupied after a period of time. Given these limitations, measurements of vacant properties may be more useful as general indicators of the scale of the problem, as of the point in time a survey was taken, than as counts of the exact number of vacant properties.

In addition, neither one of the available national data sources indicates who owns the vacant properties or whether or not they are being maintained, which would help identify unattended vacant properties that are likely to cause the most problems for local communities.[14] Not all vacant properties place the same burden on local communities. The decennial census and the ACS data categorize vacant properties in a way that makes it possible to exclude from estimates some properties that are likely to be regularly maintained, such as vacation homes; properties for rent or for sale, or those that have recently been rented or sold, but not yet occupied; or those intended for migrant workers. A final category, "other vacant," includes vacant properties about which the Census door-to-door surveyors did not find enough information to place in other categories (see table 1). According to Census officials, the "other vacant" category could include foreclosed properties that were being held off the market by the owner or were not visibly for sale or rent and may include unattended properties. This category could also include properties that fall into the other categories—for example properties that may have been sold or rented but are not occupied—however, Census surveyors did not have enough information to place them in those categories.[15] Because Census staff have used these vacant property categories in several decennial censuses and as part of compiling the ACS survey, changes in various types of vacant properties can be tracked over time.

USPS also maintains categories for residential and commercial addresses, but using these data to identify unattended vacant properties and track them over time is difficult. First, the Census data attempts to classify vacant residential properties into seven categories, whereas the USPS uses only two categories, one for vacant addresses and one category that includes vacant addresses and other types of occupied addresses, which it calls "no stat." This "no stat" category contains properties that are under construction, demolished, blighted, or otherwise identified by a USPS delivery carrier as not likely to become an occupied address for some time. The category may also include occupied addresses, such as those behind gated communities. A HUD official and other governmental and nongovernmental housing experts told us they have used the USPS data on vacant addresses for analyses of vacant properties in localities around the country. In addition, the USPS data can provide useful updates in between the Census data collection periods.

Table 1. Census 2010 Vacancy Status Categories and Definitions

According to 2010 Census technical documentation and interviews with Census officials, vacancy status and other characteristics of vacant units were determined by census enumerators obtaining information from landlords, owners, neighbors, rental agents, and others. Vacant units are subdivided according to their housing market classification as follows:

For Rent or Sale—These are vacant units offered for rent and vacant units offered either for rent or for sale.

Rented, Not Occupied—These are vacant units rented but not yet occupied, including units where money has been paid or agreed upon but the renter has not yet moved in.

For Sale Only—These are vacant units being offered for sale only, including units in cooperatives and condominium projects if the individual units are offered for sale only. If units are offered either for rent or for sale, they are included in the "For Rent" classification.

Sold, Not Occupied—These are vacant units sold but not yet occupied, including units that have been sold recently but into which the new owner has not yet moved.

For Seasonal, Recreational, or Occasional Use—These are vacant units used or intended for use only in certain seasons or for weekends or other occasional use throughout the year. Seasonal units include those used for summer or winter sports or recreation, such as beach cottages and hunting cabins. Seasonal units also may include quarters for such workers as herders and loggers. Interval ownership units, sometimes called shared-ownership or time-sharing condominiums, also are included.

For Migrant Workers—These include vacant units intended for occupancy by migrant workers employed in farm work during the crop season. (Work in a cannery, freezer plant, or food-processing plant is not farm work, according to Census).

Other Vacant—If a vacant unit does not fall into any of the categories specified above, it is classified as "Other Vacant." For example, this category includes units held for occupancy by a caretaker or janitor and units held for personal reasons of the owner. According to Census officials, the "other vacant" category could include foreclosed properties that were being held off the market by the owner or were not visibly for sale or rent and may include unattended properties.

Source: Definitions of Subject Characteristics, U.S. Census Bureau, 2010 Census Summary File 1; interview of Census officials.

However, because USPS officials told us that they had changed their vacant address data collection processes after 2006 and made other changes to their address management database in September 2010, we were unable to use their data to assess trends in the number of vacant properties over time. Because Census data enables comparisons of vacant property data over time for similar categories of properties, we primarily used Census data for the purposes of this report.

Available Census Data Show that Nonseasonal Vacant Properties Increased Significantly between 2000 and 2010

Our review of Census data indicates that the total estimated number of residential vacancies increased between 2000 and 2010. By analyzing the Census data sources, we estimated that the total number of vacant, residential housing units in the United States—excluding vacant units identified in the Census data as for seasonal use or use by migrant workers—increased 51 percent between 2000 and 2010, from nearly 7 million to 10 million (See app. II).[16] The decennial census also counted the total number of housing units, and our analysis found that the total number of residential units—the housing stock—in the United States increased by almost 14 percent during this period, from 116 million to 132 million units. Based on these data, the number of nonseasonal vacant units as a share of the nation's total housing stock increased from 6 percent to 8 percent—a substantial increase, according to Census housing statistics officials we interviewed about the data. At the same time, the number of households increased about 11 percent, from approximately 105.5 million to just under 117 million.

At the state level, the increase in the number of nonseasonal vacancies varied among states over the past decade, with some experiencing a larger increase in the number of vacant units than others (see fig. 1). Ten states experienced increases of 70 percent or more. The states with the largest percentage increases in nonseasonal vacant units over the last decade were Nevada (126 percent), Minnesota (100 percent), New Hampshire (99 percent), Arizona (92 percent), and Florida (90 percent). Census data show that these states also experienced increases in their total housing stock over the decade. For example, in Nevada, the housing stock increased 42 percent between 2000 and 2010 and, in Florida, the housing stock increased 23 percent.[17]

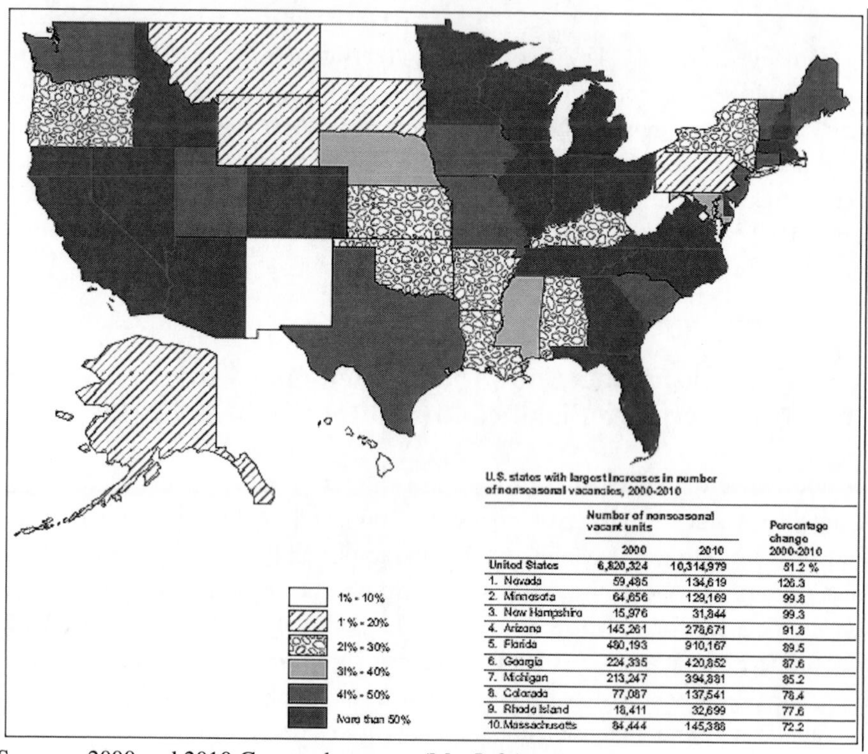

U.S. states with largest increases in number of nonseasonal vacancies, 2000-2010

	Number of nonseasonal vacant units		Percentage change
	2000	2010	2000-2010
United States	6,820,324	10,314,979	51.2 %
1. Nevada	59,485	134,619	126.3
2. Minnesota	64,656	129,169	99.8
3. New Hampshire	15,976	31,844	99.3
4. Arizona	145,261	278,671	91.8
5. Florida	480,193	910,167	89.5
6. Georgia	224,335	420,852	87.6
7. Michigan	213,247	394,881	85.2
8. Colorado	77,087	137,541	78.4
9. Rhode Island	18,411	32,699	77.6
10. Massachusetts	84,444	145,388	72.2

Sources: 2000 and 2010 Census data; map (MapInfo).

Figure 1. Percentage Increase in Number of Nonseasonal Vacancies by State between 2000 and 2010.

The Census data show that the nonseasonal vacant units' percentage of the housing stock—the vacancy rate—also increased in many of these states between 2000 and 2010, as shown in figure 2.

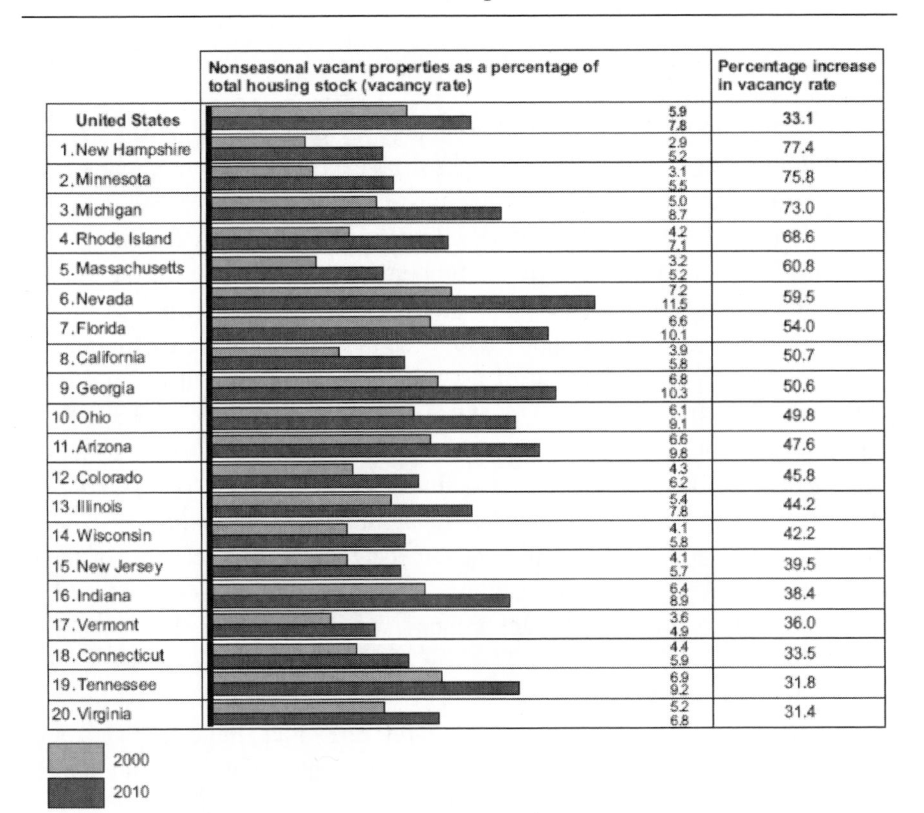

Sources: Census 2000 and 2010.

Note: Vacant units that Census identified as for seasonal use or for use by migrant workers are excluded.

Figure 2. States with the Greatest Increase in Nonseasonal Vacant Units' Share of Housing Stock, 2000 to 2010.

We also analyzed Census data at the city level and found that some cities in states with relatively large increases in the number of nonseasonal vacancies, such as Michigan and Ohio, generally also experienced increases in the number of nonseasonal vacant properties. The number of nonseasonal vacant units more than doubled in Detroit, Michigan, and increased 62 percent in Cleveland, Ohio. In both of these cities, nonseasonal vacant properties were already a larger share of the housing stock in 2000 than most of the other cities we examined—vacant properties made up 10 percent of the total housing stock in Detroit and 11 percent of the total housing stock in Cleveland in the 2000 Census. By the 2010 Census, those percentages had increased to 23 percent in Detroit and 19 percent in Cleveland. Similarly, the number of nonseasonal vacancies, as a share of the total housing stock, nearly doubled from 6 percent to just under 12 percent in Las Vegas.

Local government officials and community group representatives told us that distinguishing among different types of vacant properties is important to be able to identify the number of properties that are likely to impose costs on the community. As we noted above, the Census vacancy status categories can be useful in identifying some vacant properties, such as those in the "other vacant" category, that may be more likely to be unattended and so might burden local governments as opposed to those that are likely to be maintained, such as those that are for seasonal use. For example, prior to the surge in foreclosures of the second half of the decade, Baltimore, Cleveland, and Detroit all had large numbers of properties in the category "other vacant" in 2000 relative to the other cities we examined. However, these cities also still saw increases in both the overall nonseasonal number of vacant properties and the share of properties in the "other vacant" category as a percentage of their total housing stock by 2010. In addition, Cape Coral, Florida, experienced a large increase in nonseasonal vacant properties between 2000 and 2010—from about 2,100 to more than 11,000. Moreover, the increase in the category "other vacant" from about 1 percent of the housing stock in 2000 (433 properties) to 6.5 percent of the housing stock in 2010 (5,100 properties) indicates that some of the increase in the overall number of vacant properties in that community may have been the result of overbuilding in that city. These data are corroborated by local Cape Coral officials, who told us that many vacant properties were unfinished or newly constructed properties. Census officials also told us that such newly completed or unfinished properties would be categorized as "other vacant" by Census door-to-door surveyors. Similarly, the number of "other vacant" properties increased 271 percent in Las Vegas, Nevada, from just under 1,900 in the 2000 Census to 7,000 in the 2010 Census. Figure 3 shows the percentage of the total housing stock that was vacant (and not for seasonal use) in each time period in each city we studied, and the percentage of housing stock accounted for by properties categorized as "other vacant" in the Census data. The "other vacant" category does not necessarily capture all properties that may be unattended and imposing costs on communities. Vacant, foreclosed properties that are on the market for sale could also be vandalized or not well-maintained.

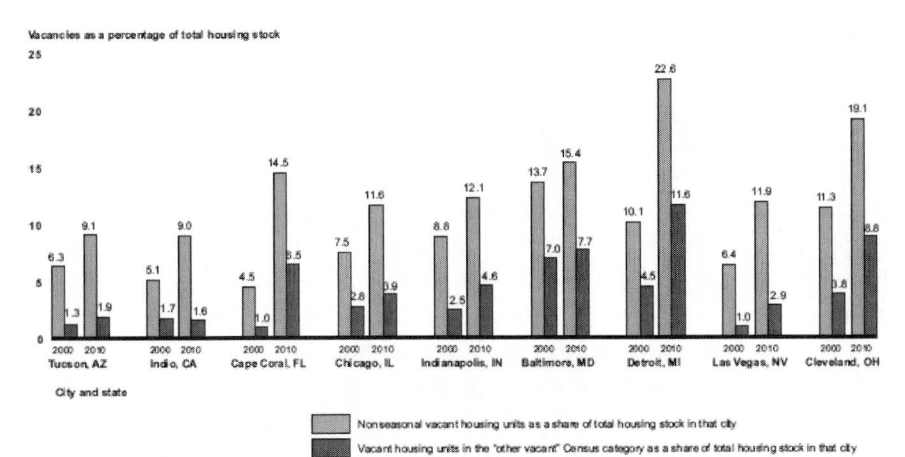

Sources: GAO analysis of Census 2000 and 2010 data.

Note: Vacant units that Census identified as for seasonal use or for use by migrant workers are excluded from the data on total vacant units in these cities.

Figure 3. Total Nonseasonal Vacant Properties in Selected Cities and Vacant Properties in the "Other Vacant" Census Category as a Percentage of Housing Stock, 2000 to 2010.

Within cities, the extent to which properties are vacant can vary substantially across individual neighborhoods. Local officials and community representatives in Baltimore, Chicago, Cleveland, and Indianapolis stated that unattended vacant properties in those cities appear to be concentrated in economically distressed areas.[18] Census data at the individual tract level—geographic divisions of 2,500 to 8,000 people—appear to corroborate these statements. We reviewed Census 2000 and 2010 tract-level statistics on vacant housing units in these cities as well as ACS data for the 2005 to 2009 period on the percentage of households below the poverty threshold.[19] This review found that the tracts with increases in the number of properties in the "other vacant" category between 2000 and 2010 were associated with higher levels of poverty, on average, in the ACS data. This pattern is consistent with our findings in our 2010 report on abandoned foreclosures, that found that abandoned foreclosures (when mortgage servicers start but do not complete the foreclosure process on a property), which tend to be vacant and unattended, are located in economically distressed areas.[20] The Census statistics also show that the number of vacant properties in such cities as Cape Coral, which is in a state that experienced large increases in new residential construction during the housing boom, increased throughout the city, but the increases were larger in the Northeast area and other areas that were developed during the recent housing boom.

Because developing precise counts of the number of vacant properties that are creating problems for communities using national data sources is difficult, various local governments and nongovernmental organizations have undertaken their own tabulations of the number of unattended or abandoned vacant properties in their areas. However, differences in data collection methodologies mean that they cannot be directly compared to national data. Baltimore's code enforcement department tracks vacant properties through its code violation system, and officials stated that city housing inspectors have identified 16,000 long-term vacant properties— many or most of which were vacant prior to the foreclosure crisis that began between 2005 and 2006—that the city considers unattended and blighted. Chicago's Department of Buildings has a vacant buildings listing of 18,000 properties.[21] The Department of Metropolitan Development in Indianapolis used a combination of data sources to estimate that the city and the county in which it resides had between 9,000 and 10,000 vacant, abandoned properties as of 2010.[22] In Cleveland, the city's code enforcement department conducts an annual door-to-door survey to count vacant properties, with its 2010 survey finding at least 7,000 vacant, distressed structures. In Detroit, a nongovernmental organization conducted a citywide survey of vacant properties and land, in which surveyors found that the city had approximately 67,000 vacant parcels as of 2009 and nearly 30,000 vacant single family homes.

A Variety of Factors is Associated with the Increase in Vacant Properties

Local officials and representatives of community groups pointed to the recent large number of foreclosures, high unemployment levels and, in some cities, population declines as factors contributing to the recent increase in vacant properties that may cause problems in their areas. Local officials and community representatives in Detroit and Cleveland, for example, stated that the foreclosures that began to increase in their cities in 2005 and 2006, and that are continuing, have substantially increased the already large number of vacant properties in their cities. Officials in Tucson and those in the Las Vegas area stated that they did not have difficulty managing the vacant properties in their cities prior to the surge in foreclosures that began in 2006. Representatives of several community groups in Baltimore stated that foreclosures had contributed to the city's overall vacancy problem, although city government officials stated that the city's inventory of long-term, problem vacant properties was due more to population decline than a surge in foreclosures.

Available data also indicate that high foreclosure rates are correlated to increased numbers of vacant properties. For example, states with high foreclosure rates in 2010, according to Mortgage Bankers Association data, also had relatively large increases in the numbers of vacancies as of April 2010, according to Census data (see fig. 4). Comprehensive data are not available on the number of properties in foreclosure that are vacant. However, representatives of some servicers and the GSEs told us that between 10 percent and 20 percent of the properties with loans in their portfolios are vacant at the time they initiate foreclosure; by the date of the completion of the foreclosure sale, they said, about 40 percent to 50 percent of properties are vacant. As we previously reported, local and state officials, community groups, and academics told us that borrowers may be confused about their rights to remain in their homes during foreclosure and vacate the home before the process is completed. [23] In addition, properties that have completed foreclosure generally become vacant prior to resale. According to representatives at HUD, for example, which had an inventory of 51,000 residential, single-family properties that it acquired as a result of foreclosures on FHA-insured loans at the end of fiscal year 2010, FHA-insured lenders are required to convey foreclosed properties to HUD unoccupied to facilitate resale. A nongovernmental organization in Chicago conducted additional surveys and research on the 18,000 properties in the Chicago Department of Buildings' list of vacant buildings and found that about 13,000 were associated with a foreclosure between 2006 and the first half of 2010.[24] Figure 4 indicates that many of the states with large increases in vacant properties between 2000 and 2010 also had high unemployment rates as of December 2010, as well as a relatively large percentage of loans in foreclosure. Nine states ranked in the top 20 for all three indicators.

The length of the foreclosure process, from initiation of foreclosure to eventual resale and reoccupation, may also contribute to increased vacancy rates because borrowers may leave their properties during the process. In some cases, the longer a foreclosure takes, the more likely a property is to become vacant or remain so, according to community and servicer representatives (see fig. 5). Foreclosure timelines are affected by the type of procedures states use to conduct foreclosures.

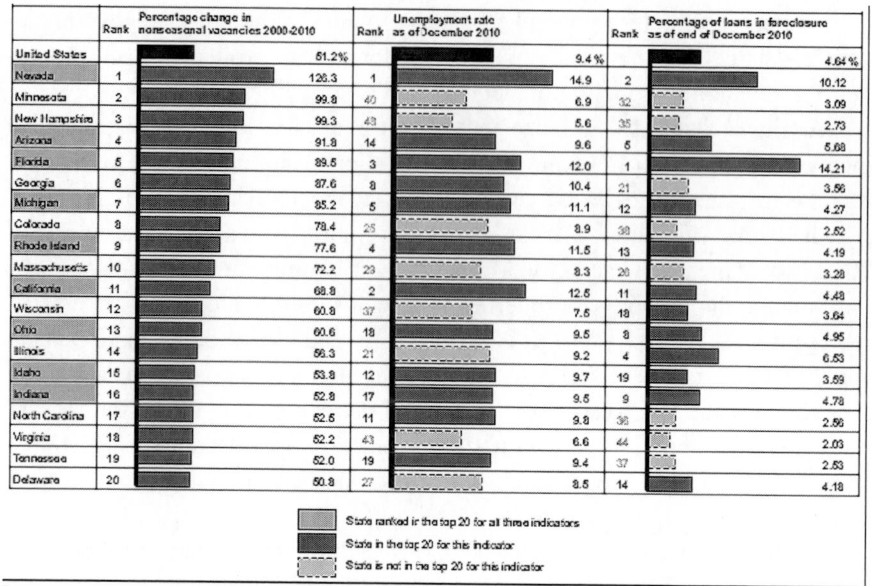

	Rank	Percentage change in nonseasonal vacancies 2000-2010	Rank	Unemployment rate as of December 2010	Rank	Percentage of loans in foreclosure as of end of December 2010
United States		51.2%		9.4%		4.64%
Nevada	1	126.3	1	14.9	2	10.12
Minnesota	2	99.8	40	6.9	32	3.09
New Hampshire	3	99.3	48	5.6	35	2.73
Arizona	4	91.8	14	9.6	5	5.68
Florida	5	89.5	3	12.0	1	14.21
Georgia	6	87.6	8	10.4	21	3.56
Michigan	7	85.2	5	11.1	12	4.27
Colorado	8	78.4	25	8.9	38	2.62
Rhode Island	9	77.6	4	11.5	13	4.19
Massachusetts	10	72.2	23	8.3	26	3.28
California	11	68.8	2	12.5	11	4.48
Wisconsin	12	60.8	37	7.5	18	3.64
Ohio	13	60.6	18	9.5	8	4.95
Illinois	14	56.3	21	9.2	4	6.53
Idaho	15	53.8	12	9.7	19	3.59
Indiana	16	52.8	17	9.5	9	4.78
North Carolina	17	52.5	11	9.8	36	2.56
Virginia	18	52.2	43	6.6	44	2.03
Tennessee	19	52.0	19	9.4	37	2.53
Delaware	20	50.8	27	8.5	14	4.18

State ranked in the top 20 for all three indicators
State in the top 20 for this indicator
State is not in the top 20 for this indicator

Sources: Mortgage Bankers Association, Bureau of Labor Statistics, 2000 and 2010 Census.

Note: This table shows the percentage change between 2000 and 2010 in the number of vacant properties, the unemployment rate (seasonally adjusted) as of December 2010, and the percentage of loans in foreclosure as of the end of the fourth quarter of 2010. The national percentage of loans in foreclosure includes Puerto Rico; the rankings do not.

Figure 4. The Change in Vacant Properties between 2000 and 2010, and Percentage of Loans in Foreclosure and Unemployment Rates as of December 2010, by State.

States generally follow one of two methods for their foreclosure process: judicial, with a judge presiding over the process in a court proceeding, or statutory (nonjudicial), with the process proceeding outside the courtroom in accordance with state law.[25] A research study by Federal Reserve Board staff found that borrowers in nonjudicial states left their homes sooner after the start of the foreclosure process than borrowers in judicial states.[26] States with judicial foreclosure processes, such as New York, New Jersey, and Florida, generally have longer foreclosure timelines; these longer timelines can contribute to foreclosure-related vacancy levels in those states because the longer the process takes, the more likely borrowers are to leave their homes. Redemption periods that allow borrowers time after foreclosure to pay to reclaim their homes can also prolong the time that a foreclosed property is vacant. According to information from an association of mortgage banking law firms, redemption periods range from 10 days in New Jersey to over 6 months in South Dakota.

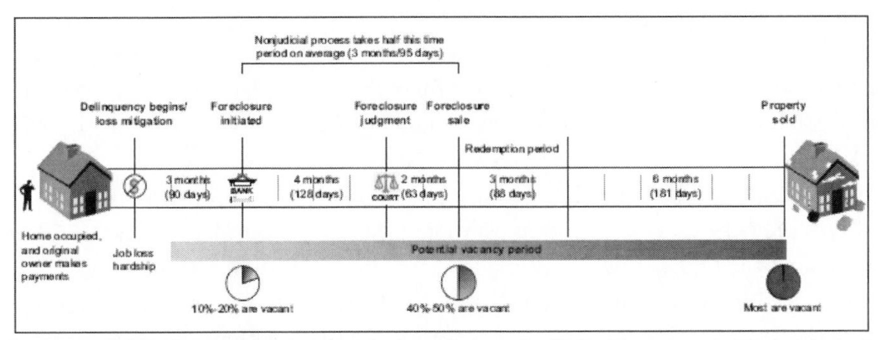

Sources: GAO (analysis); Art Explosion (images); U.S. Foreclosure Network and HUD (timelines); HUD, government-sponsored enterprises, and mortgage servicers (percentage of properties vacant at each stage of the foreclosure process).

Figure 5. Example Timeline of the Foreclosure Process and Potential Periods of Vacancy.

No comprehensive data are available on the duration of the foreclosure process or the length of time a property that has completed foreclosure remains vacant before being reoccupied; however, available information from various sources indicates that the amount of time can be significant. For example, according to GSE data, the time between the date the servicer received the last mortgage payment, and the date of the foreclosure sale, ranged from 423 days on average from 2010 through the second quarter of 2011 to 453 days on average for the first 3 quarters of October 2011. These averages varied by state, ranging from just under a year in Michigan to around 2 years in New Jersey and Vermont). Recent events and legislative changes may have contributed to the length of these foreclosure timelines. According to one report, some states have extended the length of the foreclosure process in order to provide more opportunities for homeowners to avoid foreclosure in response to the 2007 crisis.[27] In addition, we have previously reported that moratoriums on foreclosures due to improper foreclosure documentation problems at several servicers in 2010, and resulting delays due to increased judicial demands, have stalled foreclosures in some states.[28] Following the foreclosure sale, according to HUD data, HUD-owned properties spent an average of 181 days in HUD's inventory in fiscal year 2010 before they were sold. In addition, a recent research paper by an economist at the Federal Reserve Bank of Cleveland found that in Cuyahoga County, Ohio, which encompasses Cleveland, homes sold through a foreclosure sale had high vacancy rates immediately thereafter and were more likely than homes sold through ordinary transactions to be vacant up to 60 months after the foreclosure was completed.[29]

In the current environment, the length of time that a foreclosed home may be vacant has likely increased because overall housing demand is significantly lower than earlier in the decade as reflected in a variety of housing market indicators, according to government and academic analyses. For example, home sales have declined significantly in recent years, according to an analysis of two industry estimates, which estimated that home sales at the end of 2010 were significantly below 2005 levels.[30] Another indicator of low demand for housing is the decline in home prices, as reflected in two widely used indexes of house prices.[31] These price indexes show that national house prices declined between 2006-2007 and 2010.[32] For example, according to a 2011 analysis of one index, house prices declined an estimated 29 percent nationwide between 2006 and October 2010.[33] In addition, an academic research institute noted in a recent analysis that vacancy levels may be relatively high in part because the number of new households formed in the country appears to have been significantly lower over the 2005 to 2010 period than it was in the 2001 to 2005 period.[34] Further, community representatives we interviewed in two cities noted that some residents cannot afford homeownership, or are not being approved for mortgage loans, no matter what the selling price.

Recent economic conditions, including the high rate of unemployment, have contributed to an increase in foreclosures and a decrease in housing demand and, as a result, may be contributing to the increase in vacant properties and the length of time properties on the market remain vacant in some localities. Local officials and community groups in Cape Coral, Las Vegas, and Tucson, for example, stated that many property owners who have gone through foreclosure in the last 2 years cited unemployment as the reason that they were having trouble meeting their mortgage payments. As shown in figure 4 above, 9 of the 20 states with the greatest increases in vacant properties between 2000 and 2010 also were among the 20 states with the largest percentage of loans in foreclosure, and had unemployment rates that exceeded the national rate, as of the end of December 2010. Unemployed residents may be unable to afford mortgage payments, property maintenance and repair costs, and local property taxes, and may abandon a property as a result. Residents without mortgages may also be unable to pay maintenance costs. For example, one local official in Indianapolis stated that some vacant properties in that city were vacated by owners who, although they may not have had mortgages, were unable to pay local property taxes or afford the maintenance on their homes.

Another factor that can increase the prevalence of vacant properties is the extent to which they are owned by investors rather than homeowners. Investors are frequent purchasers of foreclosed homes in certain cities, including Cape Coral, Cleveland, Las Vegas, and Tucson, according to local officials and community group representatives. Investors tend to try to resell properties quickly or rent them out, according to some of these representatives. Some investors may not invest in the properties or respond to code violations if they will not be able to recoup their investments by renting or selling the properties. High foreclosures or poor economic conditions may affect the ability of investors to resell properties or to find qualified tenants who can pay rent. Investors may decide to leave properties vacant if they are unable to sell them or to rent them to a qualified tenant or may abandon them completely. Although comprehensive data are not available, HUD data indicate that about 30,000 of the approximately 88,000 foreclosed HUD-owned properties sold in fiscal year 2010 were sold to investors, as opposed to owner-occupants.

In certain cities, local officials also pointed to population declines as a contributing factor to increased vacancies. In Cleveland and Detroit, for example, the population has declined substantially over the past decade, according to Census data (see table 2).

Table 2. Population in Selected Cities and Percentage Increase in Nonseasonal Vacancies, 2000 and 2010

City	Percentage increase in number of nonseasonal vacant properties, 2000-2010	Population 2000	Population 2010	Population change	Change (%)
Tucson, AZ	57.8	486,699	520,116	33,417	6.9
Indio, CA	200.6	49,116	76,036	26,920	54.8
Cape Coral, FL	455.4	102,286	154,305	52,019	50.9
Chicago, IL	60.2	2,896,016	2,695,598	-200,418	-6.9
Indianapolis, IN	48.8	781,870	820,445	38,575	4.9
Baltimore, MD	11.4	651,154	620,961	-30,193	-4.6
Detroit, MI	107.9	951,270	713,777	-237,493	-25.0
Las Vegas, NV	137.4	478,434	583,756	105,322	22.0
Cleveland, OH	62	478,403	396,815	-81,588	-17.1

Sources: Census 2000, 2010.

The population in Cleveland declined by 17 percent between 2000 and 2010, and the population of Detroit declined 25 percent. Community group representatives in Baltimore, another city with a decline in population, told us that these reductions in population have left fewer residents to maintain the existing supply of properties. Some of these properties are as much as 100 years old or require more maintenance. A community representative stated that these older houses are expensive to maintain and lack amenities such as garages. Some officials we spoke with in these cities stated that, for economic reasons, the populations of these cities were unlikely to increase in the future. As a result, the cities were likely to have many long-term vacant properties that would have to be demolished.

IMPROPERLY MAINTAINED VACANT PROPERTIES CREATE COSTS AND OTHER PROBLEMS FOR NEIGHBORHOODS AND LOCAL GOVERNMENTS

Local Standards Mandate Maintenance of Properties, but Concerns about Legal Barriers Can Limit Mortgage Servicers' Maintenance Activities

Local governments and communities have various standards in place for property maintenance, but homes that become vacant can create problems for their communities if not properly maintained. Local governments have a wide array of building, housing, and property maintenance codes that establish standards for the appearance and safety of properties. For example, uniform building, fire, and property maintenance codes that have been implemented across the country contain special provisions for the maintenance of dangerous buildings— those that pose threats to the public health, safety, and welfare, such as structural insecurity.[35] Within local communities, code enforcement departments are largely responsible for helping ensure that homeowners maintain their properties in accordance with these codes. Code enforcement departments can typically issue fines for code violations or take actions themselves, such as making repairs, removing debris, covering windows and doors to secure properties, or even demolishing them, if needed, and bill the responsible party for the costs incurred.[36] Although homeowners are expected to maintain their properties to prevent them from becoming hazardous or negatively impacting surrounding property values, they may vacate their homes during the foreclosure process and, if the properties are not properly maintained, they can create problems for their communities. In these cases, code enforcement departments may turn to other parties with an interest in the property, such as the mortgage holder or the mortgage servicer, to resolve the code violation.

Servicer representatives and other industry participants said that although homeowners are responsible for maintaining their properties, the mortgage servicers that administer home loans, including initiating foreclosures if loans become delinquent, have the right, but not the obligation, to take on this responsibility for properties that are vacant during the foreclosure process. For example, they said that mortgage security agreements—which document that the home is the collateral for the home loan obligation and can be foreclosed upon and sold by the mortgage owner if the loan is not repaid—typically provide that the mortgage owner or the servicer contractually acting on the mortgage owner's behalf has the right to take various actions intended to preserve the value of the collateral. In particular, many home loans are sold to the GSEs, Fannie Mae and Freddie Mac, and the uniform mortgage documents associated with these loans provide that whether or not a borrower is living in a property, the borrower is expected to maintain the property in order to prevent it from deteriorating or decreasing in value due to its condition. The GSE documents also state that if a borrower fails to maintain the property or abandons it, the servicer—acting on behalf of the mortgage owner—may do reasonable and appropriate maintenance to protect the lender's interest in the property, such as securing it. GSE representatives said that this right to maintain a property is intended to allow the servicer to preserve the value of the property serving as the collateral for the loan as a way of maximizing the proceeds recovered through an eventual sale of the property to another party. According to the uniform GSE mortgage document, the types of maintenance that fall under this clause could include entering the property to make repairs, changing locks, replacing or boarding up doors and windows, draining water from pipes, eliminating building or other code violations or dangerous conditions, and having utilities turned on or off. Although servicers may take these actions under the mortgage document, they are not obligated to do so under GSE uniform mortgage documents. In addition, GSE officials indicated that some state trespass laws may contradict servicers' rights to access a property for the purposes of preservation and protection under the mortgage documents and that this right has been challenged in court.

For loans in foreclosure being serviced on behalf of the GSEs and FHA, servicer representatives said that they conduct maintenance on vacant and abandoned properties in accordance with those entities' property preservation and protection guidelines. For example, the GSEs' requirements for their servicers provide generally that servicers must be in compliance with local laws, such as local ordinances related to the maintenance of vacant and abandoned properties. Their guidance also provides that servicers should inspect properties as soon as they become aware they might be vacant and then every 30 days, or more frequently if the property is located in an area with a high rate of vandalism. In addition, they are expected to secure vacant properties to protect them from waste, damage, and vandalism and to protect their value. For example, the Fannie Mae servicing guidelines state that the servicer is responsible for performing all property maintenance functions, including mowing the grass, removing trash and other debris that violate applicable law or pose a health or safety hazard, and preparing the property for winter, among other things. Similarly, FHA guidelines require servicers to inspect vacant properties at least every 25 to 35 days, secure and protect the properties to prevent unauthorized entry, and protect against weather-related damage. FHA staff said that once properties are conveyed to the agency, they are inspected every 2 weeks. FHA also has specific guidelines on maintenance, such as how to secure properties by covering doors and windows with boards if needed, how often the grass should be cut, and what steps to take to prevent water pipes from freezing during winter months.

Servicer representatives said that for loans they own or are servicing on behalf of a private securitization trust—which are organized by financial institutions rather than the GSEs and do not have a government guarantee—and sold to investors, they follow the pooling and servicing agreements of these trusts and their own policies.[37] These agreements and policies largely call for them to take steps similar to those required by the GSEs and FHA to maintain properties. In addition, the servicers may have other policies they follow for these properties. For example, representatives of one servicer stated that the company recently implemented a policy to maintain properties "at or above community standards." Staff of another servicer told us that their focus during the foreclosure period was on mitigating any public safety issues with the property, such as a gas leak, and on remaining in compliance with local codes on lawn maintenance. Servicer representatives generally said that their goal during the preforeclosure period was to keep properties secure and prevent further damage and code violations.

Servicers that manage loans going through foreclosure on behalf of different loanholders incur various costs to maintain properties not otherwise being maintained by the homeowners. The owner or insurer of the loans typically reimburses servicers for most of these costs after the foreclosure process is completed. For example, table 3 shows the property maintenance costs incurred during the foreclosure process for which the GSEs reimbursed servicers in 2010.38 Our analysis shows that the vast majority of the costs were incurred following the foreclosure sale. Prior to the foreclosure, the GSEs reimbursed servicers $235 per property, on average, for maintenance-related expenses prior to the foreclosure sale. According to data from one of the GSEs, almost half of the expenses during the preforeclosure period were for yard maintenance and securing properties.

Table 3. GSEs' Reimbursements to Servicers and Payments to Vendors for Maintenance Costs Incurred Prior to and Following Foreclosure Sale, 2010

	Total properties	Total spent	Average per property
2010			
Preforeclosure	482,901	$113,568,550	$235
Postforeclosure	481,756	$839,973,900	$1,744
Total 2010	NA	$953,542,450	NA

Source: GAO analysis of GSE data.

Note: The totals for the number of properties in each category represent the unique number of properties that moved into each category during the year. The numbers cannot be totaled because properties moved into and out of the categories during the year, may have been in both during the year, and may have spent different lengths of time in each category.

Compared to the GSEs, FHA requires servicers to conduct additional maintenance, including removal of interior debris, to bring a property into "broom-swept" condition before transferring, or conveying, the property to the agency.[39] This type of maintenance is typically done in the postforeclosure sale period on other properties. Therefore, FHA's preconveyance reimbursements to servicers are higher than GSE preforeclosure reimbursements. As shown in table 4, FHA reimbursed servicers about $1,982 per property for maintenance-related expenses prior to conveyance to FHA in 2010.[40] As discussed above, liability concerns associated with conducting maintenance during the preforeclosure period are a significant reason for this difference, according to GSE representatives.

Table 4. FHA Reimbursement to Servicers and Contractors for Maintenance Costs Incurred Prior to and Following Conveyance, 2010

	Total properties	Total spent	Average per property
2010			
Preconveyance	89,214	$176,828,704	$1,982
Postconveyance	165,105	$38,568,420	$234
Total 2010	NA	$215,397,124	NA

Source: GAO analysis of FHA data.

Note: The totals for the number of properties in each category represent the unique number of properties that moved into each category during the year, but cannot be totaled because properties moved into and out of the categories and some properties may have been in both during the year and may have spent different lengths of time in each category. In addition, the preconveyance total spent does not include subsequent adjustments of 1 to 5 percent due to file reviews.

The states with the highest per property maintenance costs were generally those that follow a judicial foreclosure process, where a judge presides over the process in a court proceeding. Because of the additional legal work, foreclosure generally takes longer to complete in these states; therefore, maintenance may be more costly because it is required for longer periods of time.

Following the foreclosure sale, ownership of a property transfers to the purchaser and, in some cases, servicers may no longer have responsibility for maintaining properties. Properties that servicers were managing on behalf of the GSEs are transferred to the GSEs if no third party steps in to purchase the home at the foreclosure sale. If a GSE purchases a property at foreclosure, commonly referred to as REO, the GSEs manage the maintenance, marketing, and subsequent sale of these properties. As shown in table 3, in 2010, the GSEs spent on average $1,744 per property and a total of $953 million for maintenance on REO properties.[41] Most of the postforeclosure costs were for trash removal and yard maintenance (see fig. 6).

Servicers no longer have responsibility for maintaining properties that served as collateral for FHA-insured mortgages once they convey them to FHA following a foreclosure sale at which no third party purchases the home, and any state redemption period expires. Once servicers convey properties to

FHA, the agency has management and marketing contractors that conduct property maintenance. In 2010, FHA reimbursed these contractors, on average, $234 per property and a total of about $38 million for maintenance on REO properties (see table 4). Most of these expenses were for repairs, such as roofing, mold abatement, lead-based paint removal, and utilities (see fig. 7).

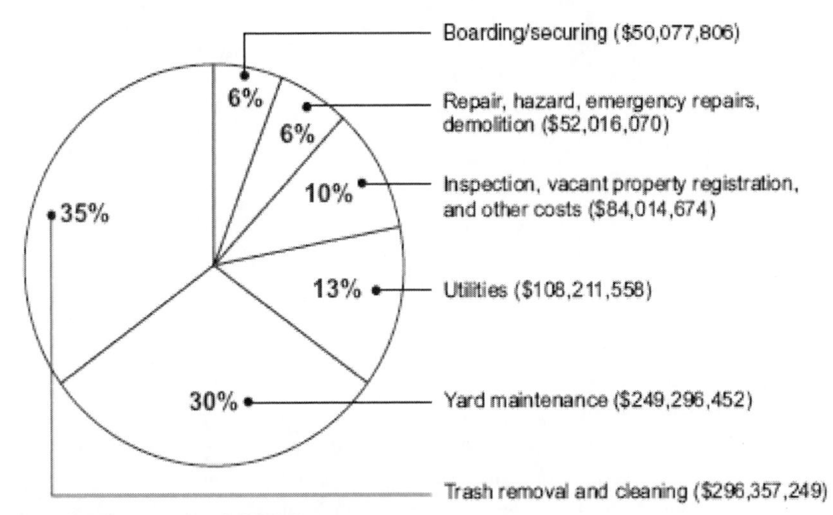

Source: GAO analysis of GSE data

Note: Trash removal and cleaning costs may include initial property cleaning and automobile removal. Yard maintenance costs may include tree removal, snow removal, temporary sprinkler system.

Figure 6. GSEs' Property Maintenance Costs Paid on Properties for Which They Assumed Ownership through Foreclosure, 2010.

In cases in which servicers are administering a foreclosure of a loan that they own or are servicing on behalf of a private-label securitization trust, the servicers are obligated to maintain the property if it is not sold to a third party following a foreclosure sale because they become (or, in the case of a securitization trust are acting on behalf of) the new legal owner.[42] When they take possession of a property after a foreclosure sale, servicer representatives reported that they may conduct work on the property beyond preservation and protection to increase its market value and therefore recover more proceeds from its subsequent sale. For example, in addition to the exterior maintenance activities, they may conduct more serious repairs, such as to the roof or foundation, as well as interior maintenance or other cosmetic changes, such as painting or replacing carpet and appliances.

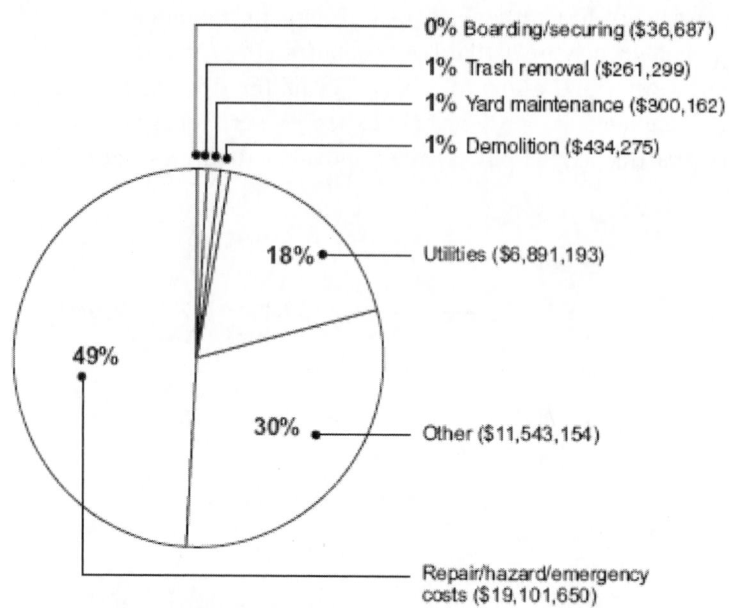

Source: GAO analysis of FHA data.

Note: Repair/Hazard/Emergency costs include lead paint removal and related costs, abatement of mold and damage resulting from a home being used to produce methamphetamine, roofing repairs, system checks and repairs, and other general or miscellaneous repairs. Other costs include costs for appliances, termite treatment, window or door bar removal, winterizing, and other miscellaneous costs.

Figure 7. Types and Amounts of FHA Property Maintenance Costs Paid to Contractors Post Conveyance, 2010.

Though most of the servicers we interviewed told us they do their best to meet local requirements and acknowledged that their organizations had the right to act to preserve the collateral value of vacant properties on which they are initiating foreclosure proceedings, local government officials said that servicers may not be providing the levels of maintenance that communities expect in some cases. For example, servicers typically conduct periodic inspections of properties throughout the delinquency, foreclosure, and REO periods and may arrange for maintenance work, if necessary, as a result of inspectors' observations. However, staff from one servicer noted that vandalism or other damage to a property could occur between these inspections. In addition, some servicer and GSE representatives told us that, prior to a foreclosure sale, servicers are reluctant to enter properties or conduct interior maintenance unless the problem would cause further deterioration of the property, such as a leaking water pipe, because they are not the owners and could be accused of trespassing or held liable for anything that was removed from the property.[43] Further, because servicers are required under the GSE or HUD guidelines to seek approval for certain unusually expensive or complicated repairs that would cost more than specific dollar thresholds, they may not always act immediately to resolve such problems. Obtaining the necessary approvals to conduct work that exceeds the allowed amounts under the servicing guidelines can take time and, in some cases, such requests are denied. For example, according to HUD officials the agency considers federal laws and regulations to supercede local laws and ordinances. Therefore, while they said that foreclosed properties in the agency's inventory are generally in compliance with local laws and ordinances, the agency may exercise its discretion to use less costly methods than the locality requires. Another reason servicers might not be maintaining properties in foreclosure up to the expectations of localities is that they have decided to abandon the foreclosure process on the property because the expected proceeds from the sale of the property would not cover the costs of foreclosure. Because a foreclosure sale never occurred on these properties, the borrowers remain the legal owners even though they may no longer live in the properties. In these abandoned foreclosure cases, representatives of four out of the five servicers we interviewed said they would not continue to incur costs for maintaining the properties.[44] In a recent report, we found that abandoned foreclosures were particularly prevalent on low-value properties and in distressed urban areas such as Detroit, Chicago, Cleveland, and Indianapolis.[45]

Following a foreclosure sale, servicers also may be limited in their actions on a property despite local expectations because of any state redemption periods. In some states, the purchaser of a property does not have full rights to it immediately after the foreclosure sale. Some states allow borrowers additional time—called redemption periods— following the foreclosure sale to live in the home and pay off the remaining amount of the mortgage and foreclosure expenses. These redemption periods can last from 10 days to 6 months, depending on state laws, according to information from an association of mortgage servicing law firms. Because the previous homeowner could continue to occupy the home and may regain rights to the property by repaying the outstanding debt during these periods, servicers typically wait for the redemption period to expire before conducting any repairs or marketing a property for sale. However, according to representatives of two servicers, they typically would conduct maintenance, such as cutting the grass, on a vacant property during the redemption period.

Unattended Vacant Properties Impose Costs on Local Governments and Communities and Reduce Revenues

When homeowners, entities that have assumed ownership of properties through foreclosure, or mortgage servicers do not maintain vacant properties, or when vacant properties are not maintained sufficiently to comply with local building or public safety standards, local governments expend millions of dollars in direct costs to mitigate the problems such properties may cause. As discussed earlier, many properties in foreclosure are vacant. For example, a recent study of vacant properties in Chicago found that 69 percent of the over 18,000 vacant properties registered with the city were associated with a foreclosure filed between 2006 and the first half of 2010.[46] In such cases, code enforcement departments may issue fines to homeowners or lien holders for code violations or bill them for work the city did to mitigate the violation. In other cases, an unattended vacant property may not have a mortgage or ownership may be unclear; therefore, the city likely would have to incur the cost of any work done on the property. For example, according to an official in the city of Newark, banks were responsible for only 15 to 20 percent of the 400 buildings identified as vacant in 2007.

According to local officials in the nine localities we analyzed, the local governments have incurred significant costs to address vacant properties within their communities. These costs were spent on tasks including boarding up and securing properties, mowing lawns, draining pools, and removing debris. Specific costs and amounts local government officials reported spending in 2010 include the following:

- *Exterior maintenance:* Minimizing the negative or hazardous impact of vacant properties by boarding up and securing such properties can cost between \$233 and \$1,400 per property in some cities. Chicago officials estimated that they spent about \$875,000 to board up 627 properties in 2010. Detroit building officials estimated the cost of boarding up 6,000 structures since June 2010 at \$1.4 million. Officials in several communities we studied also said they expended resources to mow uncut lawns, including about \$300 per property in Indianapolis, although code enforcement department officials in Cape Coral noted they had eliminated some costs by enlisting community volunteers to mow the lawns of vacant properties. A Detroit official estimated that the city spends \$25 per property for each lawn mowing on its 40,000 city-owned vacant lots and roughly 5,000 city-owned properties. Figure 8 shows examples of a boarded-up property in Chicago and an unsecured, vacant property in Detroit.

Vacant row houses in Chicago.

A vacant, unattended property in Detroit, Michigan.

Source: GAO.

Figure 8. Examples of Vacant Properties in Chicago and Detroit.

Figure 9 shows a fire-damaged property in Henderson, Nevada, in the Las Vegas area, on which foreclosure was pending as of August 2011.

A vacant property damaged by fire in Henderson, Nevada, near Las Vegas.
Source: City of Henderson, Nevada.

Figure 9. Damaged Property in Henderson, Nevada.

Demolition: Demolishing structures was another significant expense that communities incurred to eliminate the impact of vacant properties. The amounts spent on demolition varied by region and type of property. Typical demolition costs of detached, single-family properties in some cities ranged from $4,800 to $7,000 per property, according to our interviews with local officials. Las Vegas officials said the range of demolition costs was large—from $2,000 to $20,000– depending on the size of the property and the extent of lead-based paint or asbestos testing and removal needed on the property. Depending on the number of properties demolished, the total amounts spent in some cities were considerable. For example, Detroit has spent about $20 million demolishing almost 4,000 properties since May 2009—$5,000 per property. In Baltimore, local officials stated that their housing stock consists largely of single-family row houses, which are expensive to demolish individually.

A row house next to a vacant lot in Baltimore, Maryland. Row houses share walls in common and demolishing a single row house may require rebuilding the shared wall, as shown here, which increases demolition costs.
Source: GAO.

Figure 10. A Row House Next to a Vacant Lot in Baltimore, Maryland.

Row houses share walls in common, and demolishing one row house may require rebuilding the wall dividing the demolished property from one that remains standing. In addition, several demolitions on a block can lead to what one housing expert called a "sawtooth" effect, with vacant lots alternating with occupied structures (see fig. 10). Baltimore officials estimated that an individual rowhouse could cost between $13,000 and $40,000 to demolish, depending on the size and number of walls, and stated that demolishing a row of several houses at once was often more strategic, although doing so raised the overall cost of the demolition.

In contrast, demolition of a single, freestanding structure may cost far less. Figure 11 shows the demolition of a single family, detached property in Indio, California, where the average cost to demolish a property was $7,000-$9,000.

- Administrative and judicial costs: In addition to the costs of maintaining and demolishing vacant properties, local governments bear administrative costs of identifying parties responsible for vacant properties in order to assess code violation fines or liens. Code enforcement and other officials told us that it is often difficult to locate the owners of vacant properties because owners have left their homes; they also told us that it is difficult to locate current mortgage lien holders or servicers who may have an interest in maintaining the properties. Officials said that identifying lien holders is difficult because such parties often fail to record changes in ownership with local jurisdictions. As we previously reported, one code enforcement department official we interviewed allocates a full-time staff person to identifying parties responsible for vacant properties.[47] Cities that have dedicated housing courts, such as Chicago and Cleveland, spend additional resources on enforcing laws governing vacant properties through the judicial system. According to a housing court judge in Cleveland, the budget for the city's housing court is approximately $3 million.

Before (left), during (middle), and after (right) photos of detached single-family property demolition in Indio, California.

Source: City of Indio, California.

Figure 11. Demolition of a Single-family Property in Indio, California.

Although some cities receive revenue from payment of code violations or liens, as well as from other sources including federal funds, that offset the costs of maintaining vacant properties, officials in most of the cities we studied said that they struggled to pay for these activities. As we previously reported, when local governments maintain or demolish properties, they may place liens against the properties for the associated costs.[48] For example, Baltimore code enforcement officials stated that the city's boarding and cleaning costs total about $2 million per year, though the city recoups most of this cost through liens placed on properties for these costs. Not all of the cities we interviewed, however, were successful in collecting on fines and liens. In Detroit, for example, an official stated that the city has submitted $16 million in bills for boarding and has received only $100,000 in payments. In addition to the difficulty recouping costs through the collection of fines, in some jurisdictions, liens may have low priority in the foreclosure process, so that other debts are paid from the sale of the house before the liens are paid. In one jurisdiction, code enforcement liens were wiped out when the foreclosure was completed. Further, revenue from code enforcement fines and liens may not be directly returned to code enforcement departments but deposited into the locality's general fund.

Further, revenue from code enforcement liens and federal and other sources together may be insufficient to pay for all of the necessary activities, particularly large-scale demolition. Officials in Baltimore, Detroit, and Chicago, in particular, stated that the resources required to demolish the large number of long-term vacant properties in those cities exceeds local budgets. Code enforcement officials in Detroit and Chicago stated that they would use federal funds for demolition. For example, Detroit received $21.3 million for demolition-related activities as part of that city's NSP grants. As noted earlier, Detroit spent $20 million to demolish almost 4,000 properties since May 2009, and the city had a backlog of 8,000 dangerous buildings that were approved for demolition as of May 2011. A Detroit official said that the city generally demolished properties only as funding became available. Chicago planned to use $1.9 million from the city's NSP funds for demolition. Chicago officials stated that all funding sources combined fall short of what is needed to fully address the vacant property problem. Baltimore officials estimated that the city would need approximately $180 million to demolish the inventory of unsafe, unattended properties in the city. One Detroit official stated that the city's budget lacks sufficient resources to maintain the vacant properties for which the city itself has assumed ownership up to its own building standards. Reductions in local governments' budgets may also be hindering efforts to carry out vacant-property-related enforcement activities. In Cleveland, for example, the housing court's budget is scheduled to be cut by more than 10 percent due to overall budget constraints.

Vacant properties also produce other costs that can be difficult to quantify but also impose burdens on local governments and communities. For example, vacant properties can produce increased public safety costs related to code-enforcement, police, and fire services. Our past work and interviews with representatives in the localities we studied showed that vacant properties can be broken into and vandalized, illegally occupied, or used by people engaging in criminal activities, increasing the risk of fires or other public safety hazards. One code enforcement official in the Las Vegas area stated that between four and five calls per month are related to vacant property issues. Some academic studies also have found relationships between vacant or foreclosed properties and crime.[49] In some cities, local representatives stated that vandalism can occur within 24 hours of a house becoming vacant. Officials from several cities stated that they had encountered houses that had been stripped of copper pipes or wiring or electrical systems or meters, air conditioning units or furnaces, and appliances, among other things (see fig. 12). A local government official in the Las Vegas area stated that illegal occupants in properties with utilities shut off could cause fires by using alternative energy sources, such as propane tanks or candles. To the extent that problems requiring the involvement of police, fire, or code enforcement officials occur on properties in between servicers' routine monthly inspections, properties that are otherwise maintained can also impose increased costs on local governments. For example, one community representative in Detroit stated that vandalism can occur in both maintained and unattended properties. In addition, staff from a property maintenance company told us as part of work we conducted for our 2010 report, that in certain areas they had to resecure property at every monthly inspection because the properties were constantly broken into and vandalized.50 Measuring the effect of increases in public safety costs as a result of unattended vacant properties is difficult, however, because different city departments are often involved, and many localities do not routinely track which costs are related to vacant properties.

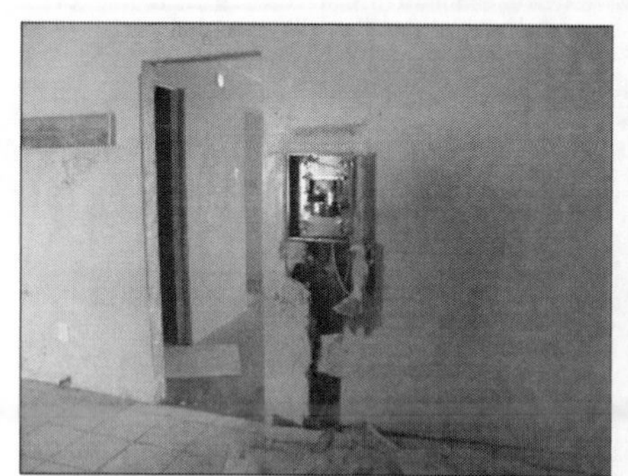

A stripped electrical box and graffiti inside a vacant property in Indio, California, in Riverside County.

Source: City of Indio, California.

Figure 12. Examples of Interior Conditions of Vacant Properties in Indio, California.

In addition to public safety costs, vacant properties reduce the values of surrounding properties. A number of research studies have attempted to quantify the effects of foreclosed and vacant properties on surrounding areas and found that foreclosed and vacant properties reduce values of neighboring occupied properties.[51] A review by a federal research organization that examined several research papers on foreclosure impacts estimated a foreclosed home within a neighborhood can depress the prices of nearby properties from 0.9 percent to up to 8.7 percent.[52] Another study estimated that, on a single block in a Chicago neighborhood, one foreclosed, demolished property may have reduced the values of 13 surrounding properties by $17,000 per property compared with the median house price in Chicago.[53] A recent study of the impact on sales prices of vacant, tax-delinquent, and foreclosed properties in Cuyahoga County, Ohio, between April 2010 and March 2011 found that a vacant property within 500 feet of another property reduces that property's price by approximately 0.7 percent.[54] The study also found that a foreclosed, vacant, and tax-delinquent property reduces neighboring property prices by almost 10 percent. In addition, the study estimated the loss to home sellers attributable to nearby foreclosed, vacant, or tax delinquent properties and found that the total value lost is approximately $76 million, with $23 million of the loss attributable to properties that are both vacant and tax delinquent. Another study that examined the impact on sales prices of nearby foreclosed and vacant properties in Columbus, Ohio, found that each vacant property within 250 feet of a nearby home could decrease its sales price by about 3.5 percent.[55] In addition, the study, which accounted for differences in neighborhood characteristics, found that the average sales price of properties located nearest to homes that had experienced both foreclosure and vacancy declined more than $8,600. Another analysis of the effects on property values in Flint, Michigan, found that a vacant property could reduce the value of surrounding homes by approximately 2.27 percent.[56]

Declines in property values associated with vacant properties and unpaid taxes on vacant properties can lead to reduced property tax revenue for local governments. According to the National League of Cities, local property tax revenues are determined by the value of residential and commercial property, based on property tax assessments that the localities conduct.[57] As discussed earlier, property values have been declining nationwide in recent years, in part because of the large numbers of foreclosures and the decline in housing demand, which have depressed national house prices. As a result, local property tax revenues declined 2 percent in 2010 compared with 2009 levels and likely will decline further in the next few years as property tax assessments are adjusted to reflect falling property values, according to a 2011 National League of Cities survey of city finance officers from across the country.[58] Lower property values might also affect the amount of unpaid taxes cities recoup from the sale of the property through the tax foreclosure process because the property value might be lower than the taxes owed.[59] Local jurisdictions also sometimes directly lose tax revenue from unattended vacant properties when property taxes owed by the property owner go unpaid.[60] Mortgage servicers typically assume property tax payments on properties during the mortgage foreclosure process, but if a vacant and abandoned property does not have a mortgage, the city may lose tax revenue from that property if it cannot be recouped through the tax foreclosure process. Further, the city may end up assuming ownership of tax-foreclosed properties, many of which can be vacant, if no other party acquires the rights to them through the tax foreclosure process. In 2009, according to the Wayne County, Michigan, treasurer's office, about 8,600 properties went through the tax foreclosure process. Of those, 7,000 were not acquired by other parties and, thus, reverted back to the city of Detroit. The city will not receive tax revenue on these properties unless it can sell them to new owners. In addition, local jurisdictions lose the tax value of a property when a structure is demolished.[61]

Local officials we interviewed in several cities stated that property taxes are an important source of revenue and that recent declines in property tax revenues have led to reductions in government services.[62] For example, local officials in several of the nine jurisdictions we studied stated that property tax revenue declines had led to budget cuts and staff reductions within their code enforcement departments. One jurisdiction provided information that showed that, in spite of increases in the housing stock in the area, housing price declines have resulted in its 2010 tax collections being equal to its 2006 levels, and an official from this jurisdiction stated that a recent effort to coordinate a response to vacant foreclosed properties was terminated because of budget constraints. An official in another jurisdiction stated that property tax revenue had declined between 6 percent and 8 percent in recent years. Community group representatives in a few cities stated that beyond code enforcement services, foreclosures and declining property tax revenues contributed to cuts of other local services, such as schools and recreational facilities. The National League of Cities report also noted that cities had cut personnel and city services such as public works, libraries, and parks and recreation programs as a result of property tax and other revenue declines. Further, a report on the costs of vacant properties in Ohio found that, because of lost tax revenues from vacant properties, the resources available to provide city services, in particular resources to school districts, were limited.[63]

The demand for and decline in availability of city services to deal with vacant properties can combine with rising numbers of vacancies to contribute to destabilizing communities, according to local community representatives. Community group representatives in Chicago, Detroit, Indianapolis, and Tucson stated that increases in vacant properties contributed to neighborhood decline because a vicious cycle is created in neighborhoods with rising numbers of foreclosed or vacant properties. Our previous work and interviews with community representatives indicated that because of the declines in values of homes surrounding vacant properties, neighbors living nearby may have difficulty refinancing their own homes and may go into foreclosure themselves, leaving additional properties vacant.[64] Increases in crime related to vacant properties could also lead to greater population loss and difficulties in neighborhood revitalization strategies. Once a block or neighborhood contains a critical number of vacant properties, the loss of population is likely to continue, further undermining the investment in a community and reducing the revenue base to support local services in those neighborhoods. One local community representative stated that vacant property problems can tip a neighborhood into decline and contribute to a loss of neighborhood worth or spirit.

State and Local Government Strategies to Address Vacant Properties Face Resource and Other Challenges

The localities we studied are all engaged in multiple strategies to try to minimize the costs and other negative impacts that vacant properties create for their communities.[65] The strategies they choose to implement are based on the conditions of the local real estate market and economy, as well as available resources, but their effectiveness is also affected by these factors. Efforts range from data-gathering efforts to more accurately identify vacant properties to acquisition and rehabilitation or, in some cases, demolition of abandoned properties. In addition, some localities have created additional responsibilities for servicers and others to maintain properties and have adjusted code enforcement regulations to create greater incentives for property maintenance, as well as establishing specialized housing courts to address vacant property and other housing issues. These local government strategies face various challenges, particularly the lack of sufficient financial and other resources to effectively address the large scale of the problem, which is exacerbated by the widespread declines in property tax revenues and housing market values, as discussed earlier. As result, governments in many of the communities we examined are reaching out to members of the community—including neighborhood groups and private developers— in an attempt to leverage all available resources and increase their effectiveness. In addition, local governments have called for increased federal funding and greater attention by federal regulators to servicers' role in managing vacant properties.

In-Depth Data-Gathering Helps Local Governments Effectively Target Resources

Local officials are attempting to address problems associated with vacant properties by engaging in a wide variety of data-gathering efforts in order to understand the scope of vacant properties in their jurisdictions, as the following examples show:

- *Compiling and analyzing data from existing sources:* Officials in three of the cities we reviewed told us they collect and analyze data from a variety of city departments—code enforcement, police, and fire—as well as statistics from the courts, such as foreclosure and related title information, in order to determine where vacant or potentially vacant properties are located.
- *Independently collecting new data:* In some cities, city leaders have involved staff or community members in data-collection efforts at the neighborhood level. As discussed earlier, in Cleveland, annually for the last 3 years, a team of city employees has walked street by street to count vacant and distressed properties, using standardized definitions and indicators of distress such as houses that are boarded up, open, or vandalized. Officials in Baltimore and Detroit hired a firm to create "market typologies" of various neighborhoods, pulling data from multiple sources—city departments, USPS, county assessor—in order to understand market strength in individual neighborhoods. Representatives from community organizations in Detroit and Indianapolis told us that volunteers collect real-time information on property conditions in their neighborhoods, compiling prioritized lists of houses that need either board-ups or rehabilitation investment.

According to the community group in Detroit, those lists were then provided to the city to use in devising its board-up strategy.

- *Leveraging resources from local universities and research organizations:* Some of the cities we studied have partnered or contracted with a local university or research organization to collect both existing data and new statistics. In Tucson, researchers from a local university conducted a survey of properties and structures (water systems, bus shelters) in five neighborhoods targeted to receive NSP funds in order to understand, among other things, the number and condition of vacant properties. At Case Western University in Cleveland, researchers developed and maintain a public website—the Northeast Ohio Community and Neighborhood Data for Organizing (NEO CANDO)—that houses social, demographic, and property data. The property data (going back to approximately 2000) were added beginning in 2005 specifically to help community development organizations and city leaders be more data driven. The data include property and lot characteristics, code enforcement actions,
- foreclosure filings, tax delinquencies, and sales transactions. NEO CANDO also has water department data on shutoffs, postal service data on vacancies, and information purchased from a proprietary real estate database, including the dates that adjustable rate mortgage loan interest rates will reset. According to a 2010 report on NEO CANDO and neighborhood stabilization efforts in Cleveland, officials from the city and local community organizations use and rely on the NEO CANDO data.[66]

These data—which can include more detailed information such as property condition and identity of the owner or responsible party, as well as aggregated neighborhood-level data, such as the number of homes with loans in default—enable more effective tracking of properties likely to cause problems, and can serve as an early warning system, so that issues can be addressed while they are still manageable, according to an organization involved in building local government capacity. However, in the nine localities we reviewed, most officials we spoke with had estimates but not precise data on the number and condition of vacant properties in their communities.

Many city officials are using these data to target their resources to narrowly defined areas in order to maximize their investments rather than putting small amounts of funds toward a wide range of communities. For example, city officials in Baltimore, as part of its "Vacants to Value" campaign, used the data from the market typology research and proximity to other nearby redevelopment projects to identify housing markets in distressed areas and to target appropriate interventions. These markets are characterized by high concentrations of abandoned properties, many of which are owned by the city or are in tax arrears, but due to the adjacent development efforts, private developers are interested in rehabilitating some of these blocks. According to Baltimore officials, the city's targeting of code enforcement efforts in these neighborhoods has assisted private developers and a local community development organization in acquiring properties for redevelopment and attracting investors in their projects. Similarly, Indianapolis and Cleveland officials told us they have targeted specific community areas that have strong ongoing community development and neighborhood organizations, with the capacity to support and bolster city investments.

Although these data-collection and targeting efforts can help municipal leaders make decisions, they can be limited in certain ways. These efforts can help leaders make informed and strategic decisions about where to make investments and to prioritize projects and needs using objective criteria (such as number of vacancies per square mile) as opposed to relying solely on political factors. Specifically, city and community representatives told us that objective, reliable data on the numbers and locations of vacant properties are important to their efforts to design and target strategies to address the problems that vacant properties produce. For example, community organization members we spoke to in Baltimore supported the city's new "market-based approach" and noted that it does not make economic sense to acquire or rehabilitate property when there is no private funding for development. However, data collection requires resources and continued updating since vacancies can occur rapidly due to continued foreclosures. Furthermore, information about vacant and abandoned properties typically must be assembled from various county and city offices, each of which may operate a unique data system. Data-gathering efforts, such as door-to-door surveys, can be resource intensive and expensive. Also, some city officials we spoke with noted that politically, targeting resources to limited areas can be difficult. Local government officials in Detroit told us they plan on using their upcoming market research to bolster their arguments for targeting funds to fewer, smaller areas of the city instead of giving small amounts of funds to all neighborhoods. However, if resources go to one area, by default they are not going to others, and those communities may still be in need.

Property Acquisition and Rehabilitation Strategies Are Also Being Used to Address Vacant Properties

To mitigate the damage caused by vacant properties, city officials and partner community organizations in eight of the nine cities we studied are engaged in efforts to acquire and rehabilitate such properties, often using federal funds. However, such efforts face declining home values, ongoing foreclosures, and sluggish economic conditions. In a typical acquisition and rehabilitation effort, a city acquires properties either through strategic purchase of foreclosed properties or by default as a result of no-sale at tax foreclosure. When feasible, these properties are then rehabilitated for a new owner or renter, usually by a community development corporation or similar organization. For example, in Cape Coral, Florida, the city purchased 82 foreclosed homes for rehabilitation and then used other funds for homebuyer assistance. In Indio, California, officials used $11.1 million in NSP funds to purchase 58 foreclosed homes for rehabilitation and resale to first-time homebuyers.

These types of city-led acquisition and rehabilitation efforts can help stabilize neighborhoods, because city leaders purchase properties with the goal of preserving communities. In contrast, some out-of-state investors, in an attempt to make a purchase and then quickly resell or "flip" properties, may undertake only minimal renovations so properties can be rented or resold to generate cash flow, according to some community organization representatives we spoke with and a study from federal researchers. One way cities can acquire properties ahead of investors and help ensure they go to owners with potentially greater incentive to maintain them is through "first look" programs, which provide cities with the opportunity to purchase properties from foreclosing owners before they are publicly offered for sale. The National Community Stabilization Trust (the Trust), which was formed by various nationwide community groups, is a national organization that offers "first look" programs within targeted neighborhoods.[67] As part of this program, the Trust maintains a database of foreclosed properties in targeted neighborhoods from lists provided by financial institutions. Cities and nonprofit organizations are given access to the listings before they become available for sale in the private market. The government and nonprofit officials are given 5 days to indicate whether they are interested in acquiring any of the homes. This "first look" window of review is offered only to cities and community development organizations, not the public or other investors. Both Tucson and Cape Coral officials purchased NSP properties through a "first look" program, and officials in Cape Coral said that obtaining the properties without the first look advantage would have been difficult, given the high level of investor interest in their community.

Another advantage of city-led acquisition and rehabilitation efforts is that the city can target its resources to areas of greatest need or where they will have the most impact. Several of those we spoke with noted that acquisition and rehabilitation efforts are most successful when they concentrate their efforts in pockets of strength where there are other investments nearby. There are rarely sufficient funds and resources, they said, to rehabilitate a whole neighborhood, but a small area near other existing assets (retail district, school) can work. For example, in the latest round of NSP projects, Tucson officials focused their efforts in older, more established neighborhoods that were mixed use—having commercial and retail sites—and therefore might attract private market buyers and developers who are willing and interested in returning the properties to productive use. Finally, rehabilitating real estate that is newer is usually more cost efficient because the costs and time needed for the work to update the property can be recouped sufficiently when it is resold.

While many view acquisition and rehabilitation as a strong strategy to combat the problems of vacant properties, lack of capacity, poor property conditions, and the large volume of foreclosures complicate efforts at the local level as follows:

- Lack of capacity: Officials and industry participants we spoke with noted that even with first look programs, government bodies do not always have the ability—including sufficient funds or expertise—to quickly complete real estate deals. Several city officials told us that, despite the importance of targeting a well-defined block or tract for redevelopment, they do not always have the ability to acquire sufficient numbers of properties within that area to make the investment worthwhile, and sometimes securing funding is difficult. For example, an official in Chicago told us that initially they had identified a block with 10 homes to rehabilitate for NSP. However, when they researched the properties' ownership, they found that the city would be able to acquire at most half of those 10 properties because of the difficulty in obtaining clear title to some of them. For example, one property was still undergoing the foreclosure process; another was a "walkaway," in which the lender had initiated but chose not to complete the foreclosure; and another had a "remote owner" who was difficult to reach. In addition, a study by Federal

Reserve researchers noted that funding capacity constraints were preventing most community development organizations from redeveloping enough vacant homes to reverse the decline of neighborhood home values.[68]

- Poor property conditions: In addition, poor property conditions can make acquisition and rehabilitation efforts costly and challenging. Acquired properties may have been vacant for long periods of time and therefore may require substantial rehabilitation. This problem has worsened as housing market values have continued to decline. With costly rehabilitation and low housing values, governments, community development organizations, or investors may not be able to recoup their costs for rehabilitating properties in poor condition by reselling them. For example, a community group representative from Baltimore said that 4 or 5 years ago, home values were high enough to support rehabilitation of properties in poor condition in some areas that bordered those in decline. Current values, however, do not support rehabilitation of such properties.
- Volume of foreclosures: While many of the city officials we spoke with indicated that the NSP program and funds had been very beneficial, the scale of the foreclosure problem in some areas is such that they are not able to get ahead of the growing numbers of foreclosures and vacancies solely through acquisition programs. Two representatives from community development organizations noted instances where they were able purchase and renovate vacant properties on a block, but by the time those properties were ready to be put on the market for sale, additional properties on those blocks had become vacant, thus reducing the value and demand for the renovated properties. Furthermore, ongoing vacancies threaten the stability of neighborhoods since the declining values and board-ups make the area less attractive for current residents, potentially leading to further abandonment and decline. For example, on a tour of a Chicago neighborhood, we saw recently rehabilitated homes that were next door to or across the street from recent foreclosures, devaluing the worth the redeveloped properties, according to representatives of a community organization working in the neighborhood (see fig. 13)

.

Another challenge to acquisition and rehabilitation efforts is a lack of ready and willing buyers, so some communities have established special entities—known as land banks—to acquire and hold properties for later

Source: GAO.

Newly rehabilitated multifamily property (left) across the street from vacant and boarded-up homes (right). According to representatives from a Chicago community development organization, the vacant homes were constructed in the mid-2000s but were never sold due to the housing crisis. They have been vacant for approximately 5 years, and contribute to decreased value in the neighboring properties, including the recently rehabilitated property across the street.

Figure 13. Vacant Properties Near Recently Rehabilitated Homes in Chicago, as of 2011.

development. Finding sufficient buyers for rehabilitated homes can be very difficult, especially in markets with older housing stock and declining populations, such as Baltimore, Detroit, and Cleveland. In current economic conditions, fewer buyers qualify for financing, and even those that do may not be willing to make purchases now as the housing market has remained weak. Therefore, several jurisdictions work with or have established a land bank—typically a separate governmental or quasi-public entity—to acquire vacant, abandoned, and tax-delinquent properties for longer periods and then convert them to productive uses, including those other than housing, such as parks or other green spaces. Land banks acquire foreclosed properties held by banks, by the GSEs, or by federal and state agencies. For example, the Cuyahoga County Land Reutilization Corporation (commonly known as the Cuyahoga Land Bank) has an agreement with Fannie Mae in which the land bank receives all of Fannie Mae's low-value properties—those appraised under $25,000—for $1, and Fannie Mae contributes approximately $3,500 per property toward demolition costs. A similar deal was struck with HUD, in which HUD agreed to give the land bank a right of first refusal on the lowest-value properties it disposes of. Currently the Cuyahoga Land Bank representatives said that the land bank receives 300 to 400 properties per year from both Fannie Mae and HUD. Land banks also can acquire real estate lost to tax foreclosure and may accept donated properties. For example, two large servicers recently established agreements with the Cuyahoga Land Bank to donate low-value properties and contribute funds toward demolition.

In communities where properties are too damaged or too low-value to be sold or rented, land banks can provide a system that enables a strategic assessment of what to do with vacant and abandoned properties and how to deal with the carrying costs of these activities. Properties that end up in a land bank may be ones that have deteriorated and may have title issues and delinquent taxes, so the interested buyers may be speculative investors interested in quickly reselling the property at a profit.[69] Land banks can break the cycle of properties moving from one investor to another who are not maintaining or improving the properties. According to a former city official in Indianapolis, land banks also facilitate partnerships between a city and nonprofit organizations. Once a community development corporation (CDC) decides to work in a neighborhood, it might not have enough funds to acquire a large number of properties, and it may be working in competition with speculative investors for properties. The land bank can hold properties, assuming the risks associated with land ownership, until CDCs have secured funding and are ready to proceed with redevelopment efforts. Likewise, industry experts, as well as officials and community group representatives we spoke with noted that a primary benefit of a land bank is that it can hold properties until the local market recovers. Lastly, land banks can help stabilize a neighborhood from further decline by either maintaining homes adequately for future development or demolishing properties as quickly as possible and tapping into other potential uses, such as urban gardens, parks, and other green spaces. For example, in Cleveland, a local faith-based organization paid for the demolition of an abandoned, foreclosed home on a lot next to its playground. The lot, owned by the Cuyahoga County Land Bank, was then donated to the organization, which planned to invest $25,000 to develop it as a green space and fill it with an amphitheater and native plants. A recent study about the land bank in Genesee County, Michigan, (discussed earlier in this report) showed that homes near vacant lots that had been created by the demolition of vacant properties increased in value.[70] Similarly, another study of distressed housing in Cuyahoga County estimated that, given an average demolition cost of $7,500, demolishing 2,000 homes that are foreclosed and vacant, tax delinquent, or all three, would net $12 million in value, benefiting sellers of nearby homes and the county's real property tax base.[71]

Land banks are not without their challenges, however. First, it could take time to successfully establish a land bank. According to a former land bank official in Indianapolis, land banks do not generate much revenue or make significant impacts overnight, and it takes a few years to establish a successful program. In some cases, localities may need to be granted the authority to begin a land bank by their state's legislature, and passage of such legislation takes time, especially in states with part-time legislators. Second, land bank officials and experts agree that securing long-term stable funding for a land bank is critical. The Cuyahoga Land Bank's primary funding comes from the county's revenues from penalties and interest on property taxes and assessments that are not paid when due. In contrast, the land bank in Indianapolis lacks an established and ongoing mechanism for receiving funds from tax revenues and instead has been funded by proceeds from liens and fines, CDBG, and NSP. Finally, some city officials expressed concerns about another entity—be it the county or a separate quasi-governmental agency—having control over land within its boundaries.

Laws, Local Ordinances and Dedicated Housing Courts Intended to Increase Accountability for Vacant Properties

City governments use housing and building codes, and related enforcement to oversee the safety of properties within their jurisdictions. With the increase of vacant properties in many communities, local governments are passing stronger property maintenance requirements and property registration ordinances aimed at increasing the responsibility of servicers to maintain properties during the foreclosure process. Similarly, two states, New Jersey and New York, recently passed laws requiring servicers to maintain properties in the foreclosure process. In addition, some jurisdictions have also established special housing courts to increase compliance with local building codes and property maintenance laws. Finally, some advocates and others have suggested that the costs of maintaining properties should be formally imposed on servicers, although the feasibility of such an approach is unknown, and it may have unintended consequences if implemented.

Code Enforcement and Liens

Municipal housing and buildings department inspectors examine properties for compliance with local code requirements either during routine inspections or when they receive a complaint about a derelict or vacant property. If the property is in violation of the required standards, the enforcement agency issues a notice to the property owner and other responsible parties that lists the specific code violations or the nuisance conditions. According to a national community-building organization, code enforcement departments work on a complaint-driven basis, although some have designed more systematic inspection programs that target certain neighborhoods or violations with fines. For example, officials in Cleveland have established a code-enforcement partnership with local CDCs in which the CDCs help survey properties in each of the city's 19 wards and prioritize enforcement needs. Through this cooperative effort, the inspection program will cover the entire city for the first time, over a 3- year period. Although the program is in early stages, its goal is to leverage the resources and neighborhood-level knowledge offered by the community organizations in order to prioritize properties in need of maintenance, condemnation, or demolition. Other city officials told us they file priority liens—which are claims on the property that must be paid before any monies owed to other lienholders are paid in the event of foreclosure—or other monetary penalties, which can be substantial and escalate over time.[72] For example, Las Vegas code enforcement officials told us that if they are unable to locate the servicer and they determine the property is vacant, they hire a contractor to perform the necessary maintenance and secure the property as needed at the city's expense. The code enforcement officials then appear before the Las Vegas city council and obtain a lien for the amount of the abatement. The council can charge the servicer up to $500 per day in civil penalties, although past responsiveness of a servicer is taken into account when the council determines the total amount of fines due. Officials in some cities we spoke with said higher fines have resulted in more responsiveness from servicers. However, another city has moved in the opposite direction, away from liens and fines. For example, the city of Cape Coral enacted a lien-forgiveness policy, which forgives outstanding liens as long as the property comes into compliance with city building codes. Officials stated that if the city keeps the liens in place, the properties would be unmarketable given market-wide declines in property values. We heard similar views from a local official and an industry representative, who said that accumulated fines and related liens can complicate the eventual resale of property by encumbering the title. Similarly, in our past work, we found that heavy fines on already low-value properties may encourage servicers to abandon foreclosure, leaving the property vacant with no party responsible.[73]

Some we spoke with expressed a concern that cities' enforcement efforts often have a "one size fits all" approach that does not reward those servicers who are cooperative and responsive to city demands. Currently, the greatest challenge to effective code enforcement in most communities is a lack of resources, according to local officials. As discussed earlier, officials we spoke with in several cities noted that they have recently experienced staff cuts in their code enforcement departments, and a shortage of inspectors can make code enforcement difficult. As discussed earlier in this report, officials in Cape Coral have recruited local volunteers to help with property maintenance, such as mowing overgrown lawns, while Cleveland officials are working with local community development corporations in an effort to expand available "eyes on the ground." Furthermore, code enforcement officials told us locating the owners or current mortgage lien holders of abandoned foreclosures takes time and money.

Vacant Property Registration Requirements and Maintenance Laws

Another action that some local governments are taking is to require servicers to register vacant properties. As previously discussed, one of the major challenges confronting code enforcement officials is identifying who is responsible for maintaining vacant properties. Vacant property registration requirements attempt to address this problem by requiring servicers to provide the city with specific contact information for each vacant property they service. According to a national firm that contracts with servicers to maintain properties, 439 jurisdictions have enacted vacant property registration ordinances as of September 2011. Although the requirements of these ordinances vary, researchers generally classify them into two types. The first type tracks all vacant and abandoned properties and their owners (regardless of whether or not there is a foreclosure action) by requiring the owner to provide the municipality with specific contact information. Among the cities we studied, Baltimore has implemented this type of registration requirement. In addition to requiring registration, some local governments have ordinances that also attempt to hold the lender or servicer responsible for maintenance of vacant properties during the foreclosure process. The cities of Cape Coral, Indio, and Chicago, for example, have implemented this second type of ordinance. Cities often impose a registration fee along with the requirement. In July 2011, Chicago's City Council passed an amendment to its vacant property registration and maintenance ordinance, expanding the definition of "owner" to include any entity holding a mortgage on the property.[74] The amended ordinance required servicers to pay for maintenance and upkeep on vacant properties before officially taking title through a foreclosure sale. Representatives from servicers and the GSEs, have expressed concern that the

Chicago ordinance went too far in assigning responsibilities to servicers prior to the completion of the foreclosure because, as previously discussed, servicers are concerned about legal liability when conducting work on properties during this period. Specifically, representatives from one servicer said the law held the mortgagee responsible for a vacant property before foreclosure is initiated, or even if the customer is current on the loan. In October 2011, a committee of the Chicago City Council recommended removing the language more broadly defining "owner" from the ordinance.

The states of New Jersey and New York have enacted statewide requirements that give cities the authority to hold servicers responsible for maintenance of vacant properties during the foreclosure process.[75] New Jersey's law requires, among other things, that all servicers notify the clerk of the municipality in which the property is located each time they initiate a foreclosure proceeding on a residential property. That way, each municipality can create a database of all residential properties in foreclosure in the community. In the absence of these new notification requirements, servicers were only required to initiate a foreclosure action by filing at a central location in the state capitol, according to a senior state official responsible for compiling these notices. This official also said it would have been difficult for municipalities to track foreclosure filings on properties in their localities using the information filed with the state. The notices must contain contact information for an entity responsible for receiving complaints about property maintenance and code violations. If at any point after the foreclosure proceeding has begun the local government finds that the property has been abandoned by its owner, maintenance of the property would then become the responsibility of the servicer or other creditors. Similarly, the New York law requires, among other things, that servicers maintain abandoned properties until ownership is transferred after foreclosure. However, that responsibility begins at the point of foreclosure judgment when a judge grants a servicer the right to hold a foreclosure sale, which occurs anywhere from 8 to 14 months after initiation of foreclosure in New York, according to a nonprofit association of mortgage banking law firms. Although the New York law (like New Jersey's) authorizes municipalities to enforce the law against servicers that fail to maintain an abandoned property prior to a foreclosure sale, it does not require servicers to provide notification to local governments. Local housing and code compliance officials in Rochester, Buffalo, and New York City told us that absent such a notification requirement, they are not able to systematically monitor the issuance of foreclosure judgments.

The contact information in vacant property registration systems can make it easier for local code enforcement officials to identify the parties responsible for abandoned foreclosures and to hold mortgage owners accountable for vacant properties, reducing the negative impact of these properties on the community. For example, local officials we interviewed in one city with a vacant property registry said that more owners are complying with their city's registry requirements due to increased fines and noted that the registry had been effective at providing contacts for officials to call to resolve code violations on vacant properties. Officials we spoke with in another city noted that because their ordinance requires certain levels of maintenance on properties, servicers have the needed incentive to keep up vacant properties to avoid incurring additional costs. They also said that servicers have been more cooperative and responsive since the registration and maintenance ordinances were passed. In addition, the fees generated by the registration requirements can help fund cities' code enforcement programs.

While vacant property registration systems can help local governments identify some owners, they might not capture all owners. Furthermore, local officials and industry representatives told us that cities lack adequate code enforcement and inspection staff to enforce fully the registration and maintenance requirements. For example, buildings department staff in Chicago noted that they do not check to see if a vacant property has been registered unless they are inspecting it already due to complaints. Several representatives from those cities in our study that do not have a registration system said there has been some local interest in starting one but cited lack of resources and staff as key impediments. Officials from the Las Vegas area said a strong local culture of property rights makes establishing a registration system politically infeasible. Representatives of mortgage servicers told us that it can be burdensome and costly to track and comply with the various standards and systems at the local level. Further, as previously discussed, servicers and other industry representatives we spoke to believe servicers' authority to perform work on properties they did not yet own was limited during the foreclosure process. At the same time, most of the servicers we interviewed told us they do their best to meet local requirements and register vacant properties as required.

Housing Courts

A few jurisdictions across the country have established special housing courts devoted to building safety and code enforcement cases. Housing courts can devote their exclusive attention to complex cases involving substandard housing and abandoned buildings brought by the city prosecutor. For example, in Cleveland, the housing court includes 10 housing specialists who work, at the judge's direction, with property owners to correct the violations on their properties. According to the housing judge in Cleveland, the benefit of a specialized court is that he and his staff develop expertise in necessary areas, such as requirements related to ownership and transfer of title. Before Cleveland had a housing court, these cases rotated among 12 other judges in the municipal court; each judge may have used a different approach, and cases sometimes languished on their dockets. In contrast, the judge for the housing court has been able to develop specific approaches to common problems regarding property maintenance and disposition. Similarly, a Chicago judge we spoke with told us his focused work in the housing court has given him expertise on all available options in the local market, and this knowledge of the history of the entities and properties involved helps him make decisions about what is the best action based on the unique circumstances of each property. For example, he might assign a receiver for a relatively well-maintained multifamily property in a stable neighborhood because that property is worth preserving, but he would likely order a deteriorated wood frame house in a neighborhood that has a lot of other vacancies to be demolished.

Another potential benefit of a housing court could be to expedite foreclosures on vacant properties. For example, the Chicago housing court is implementing a new plan for properties that are vacant, and for which the homeowner cannot be located. The judge would review the case and if provided with sufficient evidence that the owner cannot be located and has vacated the property, a judgment for foreclosure will be granted. These foreclosure cases would then proceed through the housing court rather than the general chancery court, where foreclosures are currently taking 18 to 24 months to complete, according to the Chicago housing judge we spoke with for this report. The goal of the program is to complete the foreclosure for these vacant properties in as little as 9 months, which would allow the servicer to transfer the property to an owner or entity more likely to preserve it, avoiding further vacancy and deterioration of the property. GSE representatives support the idea of expedited foreclosure, although they caution that the process for certifying that a property is vacant should not be onerous. In Colorado, a state law enacted in 2010 allows for an accelerated foreclosure process if a court is presented with evidence that a property is vacant. However, according to an attorney with a large Colorado law firm that represents most of the servicers in the state, Colorado's law has only been used in a small number of foreclosures because servicer representatives feel that the vacancy certification process enumerated in the law, which requires at least two different types of proof of vacancy such as multiple broken windows and boarded-up doors, is cumbersome.[76]

However, while a housing court can provide resources and expertise to resolve vacant property cases, in some cases, establishing such a court may require legislation, as well as substantial resource investment.[77] Even with a well-staffed and dedicated housing court, judicial proceedings still can be lengthy and costly, and depending on the responsiveness of the responsible party, vacancies and neglect may still persist. Due to lengthy court timelines, officials in Baltimore have begun a new approach to code enforcement that is intended to avoid litigation in most cases. In the past, litigation was required in every instance where a vacant building owner was noncompliant. Now Baltimore code enforcement officers can issue $900 citations (similar to parking tickets) so that the city goes to court only in cases of repeated offenses.

Servicer Accountability for Vacant Property Costs

Academics and advocates have suggested that another strategy for increasing servicer accountability and preventing negative impacts from vacancies is to have servicers acknowledge and account for the costs that vacant foreclosed properties bring to communities in the tools they use to help them make decisions about modifying a loan or foreclosing on it. These tools are financial models and calculations that generally use information about the borrower and the property to compare the expected financial benefit of taking one action over another. For example, the models servicers use to help them determine whether to offer a borrower a loan modification include factors such as the borrower's income and monthly expenses, such as mortgage and insurance payments, as well as the location and value of the property to assess whether the expected cash flow for a modified loan is higher than the expected cash flow for no loan modification. If the result of this calculation is negative, then it generally is not financially beneficial for the servicer to modify the loan.[78] Similarly, foreclosure decision-making models include factors such as projected property maintenance costs, the duration of the foreclosure process, expected time to resell the property, and the value of the property. If this calculation indicates that the projected proceeds from the eventual sale of the property exceed the projected costs by a certain amount, the servicer will proceed with foreclosure. According to some servicer representatives we interviewed, they do not explicitly take into account the costs that vacant foreclosed properties bring to communities in the models they use to help them decide whether to offer a loan modification to a borrower or to analyze whether foreclosure would be financially beneficial. One way this could be done is by requiring servicers to include vacant property costs to local governments—such as for police and fire services—in their models.

A few industry participants and observers said that adding costs related to vacant properties into the decision-making models may encourage servicers to decide to conduct more loan modifications. Because maintaining a vacant property throughout foreclosure could be more costly under this proposal, loan modifications might seem more cost-effective. Local officials told us that the high volume of continuing foreclosures makes it difficult to manage the resulting vacant properties. If more borrowers were approved for loan modifications, they would remain in their homes and prevent them from deteriorating; thus, localities would not have to expend as many resources on maintenance of vacant foreclosed properties. According to one study, any cost savings the city experiences could be used toward other local efforts to prevent foreclosures, among other things. Academics who support having servicers account for vacant property costs often being borne by communities indicated that doing so would help all parties in the mortgage transaction understand the cost of these properties to local governments and ensure that each either pays a share or takes actions to reduce these costs.

However, servicers, academics, and other industry stakeholders said that administering this proposal would be difficult. Determining the appropriate amount to add to the decision-making models to account for the community costs could be challenging, in part because of a lack of consistent data and the variation in local circumstances and property conditions. Some cities may have data that could be used to calculate the costs of vacant properties to the city. For example, a 2009 study used data from four city departments in Baltimore to calculate the cost of police and fire services associated with vacant properties.[79] In addition, local officials in Chicago told us that they have a database that tracks property information such as building violations and court proceedings and flags properties that have been identified as vacant. They said that the police and fire departments also track their costs related to vacant properties. However, many localities do not routinely track which costs are related to vacant properties. In addition, data about these costs could be difficult to obtain because it comes from a variety of sources within a city, including legal offices, public works, housing, police, fire, building inspection, and code enforcement. Determining the appropriate amount to add to decision-making models to account for these costs is further complicated by the variation in what these costs may be across jurisdictions. Although a few studies have calculated the cost of vacant properties to particular cities, these estimates cannot be applied to all jurisdictions because local housing market and property conditions vary. For example, according to one study, the effects of vacant properties on neighborhoods vary widely among regions and within specific areas of a region.[80]

In addition, stakeholders were uncertain if this proposal would be effective and said it could have unintended consequences. According to some servicer representatives, explicitly adding additional costs to decision- making models might not be effective at increasing loan modifications because borrowers can be denied for modifications for a number of reasons other than the decision-making model indicating that it is not financially beneficial to modify the loan. Our analysis of Treasury data from December 2010 shows that only 6 percent of denials for loan modifications through HAMP as of that date were due to the results of the decision-making model.[81] More common causes of denials for HAMP loan modifications were because borrowers' documentation was incomplete, the property was not owner-occupied, or the mortgage itself was ineligible.[82] According to representatives from a few servicers, including additional costs might increase the number of modifications, but the borrowers might default again because they still do not have the ability to pay. Therefore, the proposal might not have the intended effect of preventing foreclosures and keeping homes occupied. Another reason servicers said the proposal might not effectively increase modifications is that their models already address some of the costs of vacant properties. Foreclosed properties generally sell for a lower price than other properties, so servicers reduce the amount they expect to earn from selling the property in their calculations. Thus, they said that the amount that property values have declined as a result of foreclosure is already a factor that they consider and that altering the decision-making model may not result in many additional loan modifications. Several servicers also said that they account for any factors the model might miss by approving borrowers who are within a certain threshold even if the model indicates that it would not be financially beneficial to modify the loan. Similarly, Treasury officials noted that the incentives investors receive for participating in HAMP may tip the calculation toward modification, which somewhat addresses the costs to communities. Finally, servicer representatives and other industry observers said that adding to the costs of foreclosure could have the unintended consequence of causing servicers to abandon more foreclosures—that is, deciding not to foreclose on a loan and walking away from the properties. It could also increase the cost of servicing, which might impact costs to consumers or banks' lending decisions in areas where the foreclosure costs were high.

Local Officials Have Concerns about Decreased Federal Funding and Want Increased Attention to Servicers' Role in Vacant Property Problem

As discussed earlier, local governments currently are experiencing fiscal strain, and local officials told us federal funds help them address the costs of vacant properties, but they are concerned that continuing their efforts will be difficult as some programs expire, and cuts are made in others. In particular, local officials said they needed funds they could use for demolition and increasing the capacity of their code enforcement departments. Although the federal funds they receive assist in these efforts, as discussed earlier, officials in Baltimore, Detroit, and Chicago stated that the resources required to demolish the large number of unsafe and unattended vacant properties in those cities exceeds local and state budgets and federal funds. Local officials we interviewed recognized the importance of NSP funding in combating the problems of vacant properties. They said that this program provided much needed funds for demolition, and one official noted that it allowed the city to undertake neighborhood revitalization projects that it would not have otherwise been able to do, and provided leverage for attracting other sources of funding and development in targeted areas. Officials in two localities also reported that the technical assistance they received from HUD helped fill gaps in their capacity to develop systems to implement NSP projects.[83] However, this funding is coming to an end—funds from the latest round of NSP grants were required to be obligated for specific projects by March 2010—and local officials noted that it was not enough to address the scale of the vacant property problems in their areas. For example, officials in Las Vegas and the surrounding area told us they were able to acquire a few hundred properties with NSP funds, as of June 2011, but this number was not enough to stabilize the neighborhoods. According to 2010 Census data, Las Vegas has almost 29,000 nonseasonal vacant properties.

In addition, local officials noted that the ability to make funding decisions locally and the flexible nature of CDBG funds from HUD were essential to their housing programs, and that reductions in this funding would be difficult to manage. Communities can use CDBG funds for a variety of uses, including acquisition, administration and planning, economic development, and housing activities. For example, local officials in the communities we studied said that they use CDBG funding for, among other things, providing grants to homeowners to help them repair properties (Tuscon and Indianapolis), demolition (Detroit and Cleveland), enhancing code enforcement (Cleveland), and community outreach (Chicago). After budget increases in the last few years, and supplemental CDBG funding through the American Recovery and Reinvestment Act of 2009, total CDBG funding was reduced by 21 percent in 2011 compared with 2010 funding levels.[84] The proposed 2012 budget made further reductions of 7.5 percent, or $300 million, relative to current funding levels in order to meet the President's goal of reducing spending across agencies. Local officials and community group representatives from several cities said that this reduction in CDBG funding would make continuing their CDBG-funded programs difficult. With sustained high foreclosure and unemployment rates and further declining home values, local officials said that continued, flexible CDBG funding would help them maintain efforts to address vacant properties in their areas.

Local officials and representatives of community organizations also emphasized that more pressure from regulators on servicers to modify loans was needed. In particular, some local officials said that regulators could do more to encourage servicers to modify loans by reducing the principal that the borrower owes. Further, officials in the Las Vegas area noted that HAMP does not address the challenges facing many borrowers in the area who owe more on their homes than they are worth. When a borrower owes more on the mortgage than the house is currently worth, the affordability of monthly payments may not be the only consideration in the borrower's decision to stay in the house. We have previously reported that HAMP, which makes borrowers' monthly payments affordable by reducing them to the target of 31 percent of their gross household incomes, does not focus directly on the issue of negative equity that is experienced by a large and growing segment of borrowers (so called "underwater" borrowers).[85] Local officials noted that effectively stabilizing neighborhoods while further foreclosures are occurring and more properties are becoming vacant is difficult. They maintain that more pressure on servicers to modify loans could prevent additional foreclosures and vacancies. This, in turn, could allow local efforts to stabilize neighborhoods to make more of an impact. In response, banking regulators said that they encourage institutions under their jurisdiction to work with borrowers to modify loans when feasible. In addition, Treasury officials said that they adjusted servicers' HAMP incentive payments to encourage them to begin working with borrowers on modifications early in delinquency.

Local officials also said that federal regulators could do more to enforce servicers' responsibilities for maintaining vacant foreclosed properties, such as by holding them accountable for complying with local property maintenance codes and responding to code violations. Local officials we spoke with in most of the cities we studied also expressed frustration with obtaining servicers' cooperation in addressing code violations on vacant properties for which they are responsible. For example, one official said that local efforts to enforce servicers' responsibilities to maintain certain properties were not always effective. Part of these difficulties could be due to challenges in locating property owners and mortgage lien holders responsible for vacant properties. They noted that identifying the responsible party even after foreclosure is completed can be difficult because of delays or failures in recording changes in ownership with local jurisdictions. The servicers and property maintenance company we spoke with maintain that they have made improvements in communicating with local officials by setting up specialized hot lines, dedicating staff to responding to local issues, or placing notifications on properties with correct contact information in the event of problems. However, a couple of representatives also acknowledged that is an ongoing process. In response to local officials' calls for regulators to enforce servicers' compliance with local laws, regulatory staff said that compliance with local laws is expected and examiners would review whether the institution has systems or controls in place to manage compliance with local laws when circumstances warranted but typically do not enforce compliance in individual cases. For example, OCC representatives said that they do not have the resources or expertise on all the variations of local laws to review and enforce such compliance in every case.

Federal Agencies Have Recently Increased Attention to Mortgage Servicing Activities in Their Oversight

Oversight of mortgage servicers' activities regarding loans in foreclosure has not always been a major focus among federal banking regulators, although they have recently increased their attention to this area. As part of overseeing the safety and soundness of banks, the banking regulators have developed a variety of guidance that outlines expectations for banks to follow in their lending practices, loan management, and other activities, and examiners primarily structure their reviews to address the areas considered to pose a high risk of financial loss for the institutions. Federal regulatory guidance and examinations address institutions' overall policies for managing loans, not necessarily actions to take on individual properties. For example, the federal banking regulators have developed uniform standards that require depository institutions to establish and maintain comprehensive, written real estate lending policies that are consistent with safe and sound banking practices.[86] These policies must address certain lending considerations and loan administration procedures, such as inspections to monitor the condition of properties that serve as collateral for delinquent loans going into foreclosure and compliance with relevant local laws and servicing agreements, among other requirements. However, these standards do not require specific property maintenance activities. In addition, interagency guidelines for safety and soundness state that institutions should establish and maintain a system to identify problem assets, prevent their deterioration, and better ensure sufficient resources to absorb estimated losses, but the guidelines do not provide specific requirements for property maintenance.[87]

Similarly, the extent to which bank regulators have examined servicing activities such as the foreclosure process has been limited because these practices generally were not considered to pose a high risk to the safety and soundness of the institutions and were not raised as an area of potential concern in consumer complaints.[88] For example, regarding loans in the foreclosure process, regulatory officials said they expect servicers to work with borrowers to modify loans where feasible and comply with local laws, such as those related to registration of vacant properties. They also generally noted that examiners might review institutions' policies for following local laws and managing and valuing losses for the loans but would not typically review which actions servicers had taken on individual properties.

Once foreclosure is completed on a loan, federal regulatory guidance and examinations generally focus on servicers' appropriate valuation of any properties acquired through foreclosure and their activities to market and sell them within specified time frames. Generally, federal regulations allow national banks to hold these REO properties in their inventory for 5 years, but they may be able to get extensions for up to an additional 5 years.[89] According to regulatory guidance and agency staff, examiners review whether institutions are actively marketing foreclosed properties during this time period and appropriately accounting for the value of these properties. However, federal regulatory staff indicated that not much oversight is done specifically related to maintenance of vacant foreclosed properties.

Recently, banking regulators have considered the potential risks that mortgage servicing activities can pose to institutions and taken more actions regarding oversight of servicing, some of which may relate to maintenance of vacant properties, such as the following:

- OCC staff indicated that they have developed new guidance for banks and examiners that includes potential requirements and actions related to foreclosed properties. Once issued, OCC staff said that the guidance will reinforce expectations for banks to consider the legal, safety and soundness, and community impacts of foreclosed properties in their policies and procedures. As of October 2011, the guidance was not yet finalized, but was expected to be issued soon.
- Federal banking regulators conducted specific reviews of certain servicers' foreclosure activities in response to the foreclosure process deficiencies that various mortgage servicers publicly announced beginning in September 2010. These reviews revealed severe deficiencies with the servicers' document preparation and oversight of their internal foreclosure processes.[90] Regulators issued formal enforcement orders to these servicers, requiring them to take corrective actions and assess the compliance, legal, and reputational risks in their servicing operations, which include the risks of deficiencies in foreclosure activity and assisting delinquent borrowers to remain in their homes. OCC and Federal Reserve staff said that they are reviewing these assessments and expect servicers to consider legal or liability risks of vacant and abandoned REO properties in these assessments. In addition, we previously reported that regulatory staff will substantially revise their supervisory strategy to assess servicer compliance with the enforcement orders and implementation of corrective actions.[91]
- In September 2010, the Federal Reserve developed draft exam guidelines that examiners may follow that include a question on whether servicers have policies and procedures in place to address abandoned or otherwise neglected collateral properties. Federal Reserve staff said that consumer compliance examiners are testing and revising these guidelines during exams of loan modifications that were scheduled this year and have found that institutions examined so far generally have specific policies for such properties that they follow, although in a few instances examiners instructed institutions to revise their policies to make them more specific.
- FDIC issued guidance in 2008 reminding the institutions it oversees of the importance of properly maintaining foreclosed properties in

anticipation of an increase in foreclosures due to the 2007 economic crisis. The guidance notes that institutions' policies and procedures related to acquiring, holding, and disposing of properties acquired through foreclosure should ensure that their interests are protected while mitigating the impact on the value of surrounding properties. Specifically, this guidance states that properties should be maintained in a manner that complies with local property and fire codes and that efforts to maintain properties in marketable condition not only improve an institution's ability to obtain the best price for the property but also minimize liability and reputation risk.

- Federal bank regulators, Treasury, HUD, and the Bureau of Consumer Financial Protection also are developing national servicing standards. Regulatory staff could not say whether issues related to the maintenance of vacant properties would be included in any final standards. However, they said that discussions so far have focused on consumers' interactions with servicers on their delinquent loans and avoiding foreclosure, not processes following foreclosure.

In addition to federal banking regulators, FHA and the GSEs oversee various aspects of mortgage servicing and may penalize servicers if they do not comply with servicing guidelines. FHA, which oversees mortgage servicers that manage the home mortgage loans insured by that agency, uses a risk-based approach to monitor those institutions' compliance with program servicing guidelines, such as guidelines for maintaining properties. According to FHA staff, past servicer reviews have focused on monitoring compliance with requirements for assisting delinquent borrowers to remain in their homes by considering loan modifications, payment plans, or other options to avoid foreclosure. To provide incentives for servicers to maintain properties according to the agency's guidelines prior to transferring them to HUD following the foreclosure sale, the agency may deny or curtail insurance claims or reconvey a property if it does not meet certain conveyance requirements. As previously discussed, these properties are generally in compliance with local laws and ordinances, but HUD officials told us that the agency may exercise its discretion to use different methods than the locality requires. Representatives from the GSEs also reported that they conduct targeted reviews of servicers that focus on evaluating their processes and procedures. They said that they require servicers to follow servicing guidelines and proper legal procedures with respect to all aspects of their business operations as part of their contractual obligations with the GSEs. They also may pursue a variety of remedies, such as assessing fees or penalties on servicers, for failure to comply with the servicing guidelines, but said that they did not assess fees for maintenance-related issues. Instead, Fannie Mae officials said that, in cases of properties damaged because of the servicer's neglect, they may require the servicer to repurchase the property or reimburse Fannie Mae for any loss in the property's value. GSE representatives also noted that they train and routinely monitor the vendors that manage their REO properties to ensure that they comply with local laws and have third-party companies review their performance.

FHFA and the GSEs also are evaluating future measures to improve mortgage servicing. At the direction of their regulator, FHFA, the GSEs are working together to align their guidelines to servicers to establish, among other things, consistent timelines and other requirements.[92] In addition, FHFA, in consultation with Treasury and HUD, is seeking input for planning and market research purposes on new options for selling REO properties held by Fannie Mae, Freddie Mac, and FHA to reduce GSE and FHA losses on foreclosed properties and help stabilize neighborhoods. Options the agencies requested comments on include renting REO properties to previous homeowners or other parties or facilitating current tenants becoming owners. The notice stated that areas with a substantial number of REO properties and a strong rental market may begin to stabilize by turning a large number of REO properties into rental housing.[93] FHFA is in the process of reviewing comments on such alternatives, including their risks and any trade-offs involved.

As part of the HAMP program, Treasury oversees participating servicers' compliance with their contractual obligations under the program. Treasury conducts compliance audits on all servicers that participate in the program according to a risk-based schedule. In addition, as a consequence of reported irregularities in the foreclosure process in September 2010, Treasury organized a review of the internal policies and procedures governing preforeclosure activities at the certain servicers and reiterated servicers' obligations to follow applicable state laws. Our previous work on HAMP has shown that Treasury had not finalized policies to hold servicers accountable for their performance, although Treasury has recently begun publishing assessments of the performance of the 10 largest servicers and, as of July 2011, is withholding incentive payments that servicers receive for making loan modifications from two servicers until they make substantial improvements in their programs.[94] Further, we have found that servicers were not always consistent in their treatment of borrowers applying for loan modifications.[95] We have made a number of recommendations to Treasury to help ensure that borrowers are treated consistently and servicers are held accountable for their performance, which we will continue to monitor.

Agency Comments and Our Evaluation

We requested comments on a draft of this report from the Federal Reserve, Census, HUD, Treasury, Fannie Mae, FDIC, FHFA, Freddie Mac, OCC, and USPS. We received technical comments from Census, Federal Reserve, FHFA, Fannie Mae, Freddie Mac, OCC, and FHA, which we incorporated where appropriate.

The Assistant Secretary for Financial Stability at the Department of the Treasury noted that the report is informative and helpful in describing the extent of vacant properties and their impacts. One of the strategies discussed in our report is requiring servicers to include vacant property costs to local governments—such as for police and fire services—into the models used to make loan modification or foreclosure decisions. The Assistant Secretary's letter acknowledges, as we noted in the report, that there are certain challenges associated with holding servicers accountable for such costs. The Assistant Secretary's letter also states that federal, state, and local agencies as well as community groups, investors, and servicers need to analyze appropriate responses to this issue.

Sincerely yours,
Mathew J. Scirè Director
Financial Markets and Community Investment

APPENDIX I. OBJECTIVES, SCOPE, AND METHODOLOGY

This report reviews the costs that foreclosed and unattended vacant homes create for local communities and the strategies state and local governments are using to address problems associated with unattended vacant properties. Specifically, this report addresses (1) trends in the number of vacant properties and how they relate to the recent increase in foreclosures; (2) the types of costs that vacant properties create and who bears the responsibility for these properties and their costs; and (3) state and local government strategies for addressing vacant properties and the federal role in assisting these efforts.

To identify trends in the number of vacant properties and how they relate to the recent increase in foreclosures, we analyzed data on vacant residential housing units collected in the 2000 and 2010 decennial censuses. In order to describe the extent of and change in housing vacancies across states and selected cities from 2000 through 2010, we estimated the number of vacancies in 2000 and 2010 to show the trend in vacancies over the decade. We estimated the change in total vacancies and the number of vacancies as a percentage of the total housing stock between the two censuses. We excluded vacant units that Census categorized as for seasonal use or for use by migrant workers because we concluded that these properties, which are generally occupied for temporary periods, are likely to be maintained.

We downloaded census data from Census 2000 and the 2010 Census from the Census Bureau's American FactFinder. These data contain the occupancy status of enumerated households and describe the reason for the vacancy. The vacancy status is defined as for rent or sale; for sale only; rented or sold, not occupied; for seasonal, recreational, or occasional use; for migrant workers; and other vacant.

In addition, we analyzed data compiled from the U.S. Postal Service (USPS) on vacant addresses as of the second quarter of 2010 to compare it with Census 2010 data on vacant properties, as a check on Census data as well as to highlight any interesting characteristics that the Census data may not identify.

We tabulated the total number of residential vacant addresses at national and state levels, subtracting out seasonal addresses, and calculated the percentage difference for each state and the average difference. We did not report the results of the comparison because of the differences in methodology and definitions between the two sets of data.

We did report our comparison of the 10 states with the largest number of vacant addresses according to USPS second quarter 2010 data and the 10 states with the largest number of nonseasonal residential vacant units according to Census 2010 data.

Users of the report should note that accurately measuring the number of vacant properties is difficult and that available data all have limitations. The primary difficulty is identifying whether a property is actually vacant, which generally is done through physical inspection of property exteriors, information from neighbors, or reviews of public utility usage or billing records.

No comprehensive data are available about the duration that properties are vacant. As a result, measurements of vacant properties should be viewed as general indicators of the scale of the problem as of the point in time the given survey was taken.

In light of these limitations, we assessed the reliability of the Census and USPS data by reviewing past GAO and other assessments of the data and interviewing knowledgeable Census and USPS officials about their data integrity measures.[1] We determined that these data were sufficiently reliable for use in the report.

To identify the factors that contributed to the increase in vacant properties over the last decade, we evaluated data on foreclosures, unemployment, and population. Specifically, we analyzed data on foreclosure inventory by state as of the end of 2010 from the Mortgage Bankers Association National Delinquency Survey. In a previous report released earlier this year, we assessed the reliability of these same data by reviewing existing information about the quality of the data, a previous GAO data reliability assessment that included performing electronic testing to detect errors in completeness and reasonableness, and interviewing Mortgage Bankers Association officials knowledgeable about the data to confirm that the data collection methodology had not changed since our earlier review.[2] We determined that the data were sufficiently reliable for purposes of the report. We obtained data on unemployment and population from the Bureau of Labor Statistics and Census.

The federal statistical agencies of the U.S. government follow the standards and guidelines for statistical surveys set forth by the Office of Management and Budget.

These standards and guidelines governing federal statistical agencies are intended to help ensure that their surveys and studies are designed to produce reliable data as efficiently as possible and that their methods are documented and results presented in a manner that makes the data as accessible and useful as possible. In addition, we reviewed literature on the effects of foreclosures and vacant properties on property values.

We also interviewed local government and nongovernmental officials about the factors contributing to properties becoming vacant in their areas. To further corroborate the association between increases in the number of vacant housing units categorized as “other vacant” between the 2000 and 2010 censuses, and areas of economic distress, we analyzed data from the Census American Community Survey (ACS) for the period 2005 through 2009 on the percentage of households in a given census tract with annual income below the appropriate poverty threshold for that household size and composition as defined by the Census Bureau.[3]

We used the ACS data because 2010 poverty data was not yet available at the time we undertook this analysis. ACS data at the tract level can be unreliable for reporting for some tracts but the data were sufficiently reliable for the type of aggregate analysis we conducted.

To understand the costs that mortgage servicers and lien holders bear to maintain vacant properties during and after foreclosure, we analyzed data on property maintenance costs from two housing-related government-sponsored enterprises (GSE)—Fannie Mae and Freddie Mac—and HUD's Federal Housing Administration (FHA).

Specifically, we obtained data on the funds the GSEs and FHA reimbursed to servicers for maintenance of single-family properties secured by GSE-guaranteed and FHA-insured loans during the foreclosure process from 2005 through 2010.

We also obtained data on the payments GSEs made to third-party contractors for properties in their possession following foreclosure, for the years 2005 through 2010.

We obtained data from HUD on the payments made to third-party contractors for fiscal years 2005 and 2010 and the first half of fiscal year 2011 for maintenance of HUD-owned, single-family properties. To assess the reliability of these data, we reviewed available documentation and interviewed knowledgeable GSE and HUD officials. We determined that the data were sufficiently reliable for use in the report.

To understand the specific costs incurred by localities and strategies some localities have taken to address these costs, we reviewed relevant literature and conducted case studies of specific locations. We reviewed academic and other reports on the effects of vacant and foreclosed properties on local communities, strategies being used to address these issues, and the recent trends in fiscal conditions among states and cities.

We categorized the information we gathered from these various sources to identify the most common types of strategies and their advantages and disadvantages. We also selected nine locations from different regions of the country, which had a range of

1) experiences with vacant properties, including different costs for maintaining vacant properties;
2) experiences with foreclosures, including states with judicial and nonjudicial foreclosure processes;
3) economic conditions, such as unemployment rates; and

4) HUD evaluations of need for funds under the Neighborhood Stabilization Program (NSP) and HUD assessments of use of NSP funds.

In addition, we identified from our literature search locations that were taking innovative approaches to the vacant property problem. We selected Baltimore, Maryland; Cape Coral, Florida; Chicago, Illinois; Cleveland, Ohio; Detroit, Michigan; Indianapolis, Indiana; Indio, California; Las Vegas, Nevada; and Tucson, Arizona.

We conducted in-person site visits to four locations and conducted telephone interviews in other cities with local government officials and representatives of nonprofit and community development organizations. In addition, we interviewed code enforcement officials about the impact of state laws in New York and New Jersey, states that recently enacted laws related to the maintenance of vacant properties in foreclosure. Although we selected these locations to provide broad representation of conditions related to vacant properties, these locations may not necessarily be representative of all localities nationwide.

As a result, we could not generalize the results of our analysis to all states and localities. Officials in two of the locations provided us with pictures and examples of vacant properties. In site visits to Baltimore, Chicago, the Las Vegas area, and Tucson, and during prior visits to Cape Coral and Detroit, we visited selected vacant and foreclosed properties and took pictures to document examples of property conditions.

To inform our work on each of these objectives, we also conducted other interviews. We interviewed staff from one of the largest maintenance companies that conducts property inspections and maintenance on behalf of services nationwide, academic researchers, GSE staff, and five mortgage servicers—including some of the largest firms and those that specialized in subprime loans.

In addition, we interviewed representatives of federal agencies, including the Board of Governors of the Federal Reserve System (Federal Reserve), Federal Deposit Insurance Corporation (FDIC), Office of the Comptroller of the Currency (OCC), Department of Housing and Urban Development (HUD), Federal Housing Finance Agency (FHFA), and Treasury.

We conducted this performance audit from November 2010 through November 2011 in accordance with generally accepted government auditing standards.

Those standards require that we plan and perform the audit to obtain sufficient, appropriate evidence to provide a reasonable basis for our findings and conclusions based on our audit objectives. We believe that the evidence obtained provides a reasonable basis for our findings and conclusions based on our audit objectives.

APPENDIX II. U.S. DECENNIAL CENSUS DATA ON RESIDENTIAL VACANCIES, 2000 AND 2010

The data below were compiled from Census 2000 and 2010 on residential vacancies and are available through the U.S. Census Bureau's American FactFinder website. Table 5 shows total housing units, total vacancies, and vacancies by category. These categories include vacant units for rent or sale; for sale only; for seasonal, recreational, or occasional use; for migrant workers; or other.

The 2000 Census used a category of vacant units called "rented or sold, not occupied" while the 2010 Census used separate categories for vacant units identified as "rented, not occupied" and "sold, not occupied." We combined those two categories for 2010 for comparative purposes. Table 5 also shows the share of the total housing stock that was vacant in each time period, for all vacancies, as well as nonseasonal vacancies, which excludes those used seasonally or for migrant workers.

The table shows the percentage change between 2000 and 2010 for each category of data. Census data do not distinguish between single- and multiunit residential properties.

Table 5. Census Data on Vacant Residential Units, 2000 and 2010

State	Year	Housing units	Total vacancies	For rent or sale	For sale only	Rented or sold, not occupied	For seasonal, recreational, or occasional use	For migrant workers	Other vacant	Total nonseasonal vacant units	Vacant units' share of housing stock	Nonseasonal vacant units' share of housing stock
United States	2010	131,704,730	14,988,438	4,137,567	1,896,796	627,857	4,649,298	24,161	3,652,759	10,314,979	11.4	7.8
	2000	115,904,641	10,424,540	2,614,652	1,204,318	702,435	3,578,718	25,498	2,298,919	6,820,324	9.0	5.9
Percent change	2000-2010	13.6%	43.8	58.2	57.5	-10.6	29.9	-5.2	58.9	51.2	26.5	33.1
Alabama	2010	2,171,853	288,062	79,265	35,903	12,988	63,890	238	95,778	223,934	13.3	10.3
	2000	1,963,711	226,631	64,091	25,858	15,560	47,205	369	73,548	179,057	11.5	9.1
Percent change	2000-2010	10.6%	27.1	23.7	38.8	-16.5	35.3	-35.5	30.2	25.1	14.9	13.1
Alaska	2010	306,967	48,909	6,729	2,876	1,673	27,901	362	9,368	20,646	15.9	6.7
	2000	260,978	39,378	7,036	2,612	2,066	21,474	180	6,010	17,724	15.1	6.8
Percent change	2000-2010	17.6%	24.2	-4.4	10.1	-19.0	29.9	101.1	55.9	16.5	5.6	-1.0
Arizona	2010	2,844,526	463,536	120,490	64,407	15,999	184,327	538	77,775	278,671	16.3	9.8
	2000	2,189,189	287,862	61,781	27,775	12,679	141,965	636	43,026	145,261	13.1	6.6
Percent change	2000-2010	29.9%	61.0	95.0	131.9	26.2	29.8	-15.4	80.8	91.8	23.9	47.6
Arkansas	2010	1,316,299	169,215	46,443	18,500	7,134	38,153	345	58,640	130,717	12.9	9.9
	2000	1,173,043	130,347	33,740	18,238	8,974	29,012	377	40,006	100,958	11.1	8.6
Percent change	2000-2010	12.2%	29.8	37.6	1.4	-20.5	31.5	-8.5	46.6	29.5	15.7	15.4
California	2010	13,680,081	1,102,583	374,610	154,775	54,635	302,815	2,100	213,648	797,668	8.1	5.8
	2000	12,214,549	711,679	190,321	92,197	50,846	236,857	2,205	139,253	472,617	5.8	3.9
Percent	2000-	12.0%	54.9	96.8	67.9	7.5	27.8	-4.8	53.4	68.8	38.3	50.7

State	Year	Housing units	Total vacancies	For rent or sale	For sale only	Rented or sold, not occupied	For seasonal, recreational, or occasional use	For migrant workers	Other vacant	Total nonseasonal vacant units	Vacant units' share of housing stock	Nonseasonal vacant units' share of housing stock
change	2010											
Colorado	2010	2,212,898	240,030	57,644	32,673	8,476	101,965	524	38,748	137,541	10.8	6.2
	2000	1,808,037	149,799	31,852	16,142	8,116	72,263	449	20,977	77,087	8.3	4.3
Percent change	2000-2010	22.4%	60.2	81.0	102.4	4.4	41.1	16.7	84.7	78.4	30.9	45.8
Connecticut	2010	1,487,891	116,804	40,004	15,564	5,689	29,618	55	25,874	87,131	7.9	5.9
	2000	1,385,975	84,305	25,575	9,305	6,320	23,379	138	19,588	60,788	6.1	4.4
Percent change	2000-2010	7.4%	38.5	56.4	67.3	-10.0	26.7	-60.1	32.1	43.3	29.1	33.5
Delaware	2010	405,885	63,588	11,399	5,985	1,687	35,939	43	8,535	27,606	15.7	6.8
	2000	343,072	44,336	7,393	3,273	1,693	25,977	53	5,947	18,306	12.9	5.3
Percent change	2000-2010	18.3%	43.4	54.2	82.9	-0.4	38.3	-18.9	43.5	50.8	21.2	27.5
District of Columbia	2010	296,719	30,012	13,393	3,930	1,933	3,537	8	7,211	26,467	10.1	8.9
	2000	274,845	26,507	9,202	3,021	2,667	2,207	47	9,363	24,253	9.6	8.8
Percent change	2000-2010	8.0%	13.2	45.5	30.1	-27.5	60.3	-83.0	-23.0	9.1	4.9	1.1
Florida	2010	8,989,580	1,568,778	371,626	198,232	47,349	657,070	1,541	292,960	910,167	17.5	10.1
	2000	7,302,947	965,018	195,336	101,667	53,429	482,944	1,881	129,761	480,193	13.2	6.6
Percent change	2000-2010	23.1%	62.6	90.2	95.0	-11.4	36.1	-18.1	125.8	89.5	32.1	54.0
Georgia	2010	4,088,801	503,217	174,416	83,852	19,910	81,511	854	142,674	420,852	12.3	10.3
	2000	3,281,737	275,368	86,905	38,440	20,353	50,064	969	78,637	224,335	8.4	6.8

Table 5. (Continued)

State	Year	Housing units	Total vacancies	For rent or sale	For sale only	Rented or sold, not occupied	For seasonal, recreational, or occasional use	For migrant workers	Other vacant	Total nonseasonal vacant units	Vacant units' share of housing stock	Nonseasonal vacant units' share of housing stock
Percent change	2000-2010	24.6%	82.7	100.7	118.1	-2.2	62.8	-11.9	81.4	87.6	46.7	50.6
Hawaii	2010	519,508	64,170	16,441	4,277	2,105	30,079	117	11,151	33,974	12.4	6.5
	2000	460,542	57,302	15,699	3,720	2,683	25,584	57	9,559	31,661	12.4	6.9
Percent change	2000-2010	12.8%	12.0	4.7	15.0	-21.5	17.6	105.3	16.7	7.3	-0.7	-4.9
Idaho	2010	667,796	88,388	16,360	12,814	3,174	41,660	632	13,748	46,096	13.2	6.9
	2000	527,824	58,179	10,656	7,682	2,725	27,478	721	8,917	29,980	11.0	5.7
Percent change	2000-2010	26.5%	51.9	53.5	66.8	16.5	51.6	-12.3	54.2	53.8	20.1	21.5
Illinois	2010	5,296,715	459,743	158,882	82,739	24,675	47,289	315	145,843	412,139	8.7	7.8
	2000	4,885,615	293,836	99,019	46,896	31,689	29,712	407	86,113	263,717	6.0	5.4
Percent change	2000-2010	8.4%	56.5	60.5	76.4	-22.1	59.2	-22.6	69.4	56.3	44.3	44.2
Indiana	2010	2,795,541	293,387	93,029	46,410	14,721	45,571	200	93,456	247,616	10.5	8.9
	2000	2,532,319	196,013	64,363	29,816	17,432	33,803	179	50,420	162,031	7.7	6.4
Percent change	2000-2010	10.4%	49.7	44.5	55.7	-15.6	34.8	11.7	85.4	52.8	35.6	38.4
Iowa	2010	1,336,417	114,841	31,812	18,405	7,358	21,020	87	36,159	93,734	8.6	7.0
	2000	1,232,511	83,235	23,272	14,067	7,444	16,472	77	21,903	66,686	6.8	5.4
Percent change	2000-2010	8.4%	38.0	36.7	30.8	-1.2	27.6	13.0	65.1	40.6	27.2	29.6
Kansas	2010	1,233,215	121,119	40,445	16,286	7,229	12,763	129	44,267	108,227	9.8	8.8
	2000	1,131,200	93,309	30,940	14,821	7,845	9,639	137	29,927	83,533	8.2	7.4
Percent	2000-	9.0%	29.8	30.7	9.9	-7.9	32.4	-5.8	47.9	29.6	19.1	18.8

State	Year	Housing units	Total vacancies	For rent or sale	For sale only	Rented or sold, not occupied	For seasonal, recreational, or occasional use	For migrant workers	Other vacant	Total nonseasonal vacant units	Vacant units' share of housing stock	Nonseasonal vacant units' share of housing stock
change	2010											
Kentucky	2010	1,927,164	207,199	56,960	27,286	11,746	38,616	627	71,964	167,956	10.8	8.7
	2000	1,750,927	160,280	44,268	20,748	13,421	30,420	715	50,708	129,145	9.2	7.4
Percent change	2000-2010	10.1%	29.3	28.7	31.5	-12.5	26.9	-12.3	41.9	30.1	17.5	18.2
Louisiana	2010	1,964,981	236,621	66,857	21,480	10,567	42,253	999	94,465	193,369	12.0	9.8
	2000	1,847,181	191,128	54,185	18,097	18,144	39,578	525	60,599	151,025	10.3	8.2
Percent change	2000-2010	6.4%	23.8	23.4	18.7	-41.8	6.8	90.3	55.9	28.0	16.4	20.4
Maine	2010	721,830	164,611	15,738	9,711	3,110	118,310	160	17,582	46,141	22.8	6.4
	2000	651,901	133,701	11,153	6,249	3,569	101,470	70	11,190	32,161	20.5	4.9
Percent change	2000-2010	10.7%	23.1	41.1	55.4	-12.9	16.6	128.6	57.1	43.5	11.2	29.6
Maryland	2010	2,378,814	222,403	61,874	32,883	10,328	55,786	177	61,355	166,440	9.3	7.0
	2000	2,145,283	164,424	41,751	22,375	12,492	38,880	167	48,759	125,377	7.7	5.8
Percent change	2000-2010	10.9%	35.3	48.2	47.0	-17.3	43.5	6.0	25.8	32.8	22.0	19.7
Massachusetts	2010	2,808,254	261,179	66,673	25,038	10,230	115,630	161	43,447	145,388	9.3	5.2
	2000	2,621,989	178,409	34,174	10,861	9,218	93,771	194	30,191	84,444	6.8	3.2
Percent change	2000-2010	7.1%	46.4	95.1	130.5	11.0	23.3	-17.0	43.9	72.2	36.7	60.8
Michigan	2010	4,532,233	659,725	141,687	77,080	24,662	263,071	1,773	151,452	394,881	14.6	8.7
	2000	4,234,279	448,618	72,805	44,250	27,161	233,922	1,449	69,031	213,247	10.6	5.0
Percent change	2000-2010	7.0%	47.1	94.6	74.2	-9.2	12.5	22.4	119.4	85.2	37.4	73.0

Table 5. (Continued)

State	Year	Housing units	Total vacancies	For rent or sale	For sale only	Rented or sold, not occupied	For seasonal, recreational, or occasional use	For migrant workers	Other vacant	Total nonseasonal vacant units	Vacant units' share of housing stock	Nonseasonal vacant units' share of housing stock
Minnesota	2010	2,347,201	259,974	48,091	30,726	9,430	130,471	334	40,922	129,169	11.1	5.5
	2000	2,065,946	170,819	20,452	13,392	8,022	105,609	554	22,790	64,656	8.3	3.1
Percent change	2000-2010	13.6%	52.2	135.1	129.4	17.6	23.5	-39.7	79.6	99.8	34.0	75.8
Mississippi	2010	1,274,719	158,951	44,735	16,886	6,835	28,867	318	61,310	129,766	12.5	10.2
	2000	1,161,953	115,519	29,486	12,456	10,035	21,845	299	41,398	93,375	9.9	8.0
Percent change	2000-2010	9.7%	37.6	51.7	35.6	-31.9	32.1	6.4	48.1	39.0	25.4	26.7
Missouri	2010	2,712,729	337,118	92,946	44,200	15,388	80,374	193	104,017	256,551	12.4	9.5
	2000	2,442,017	247,423	64,167	33,775	18,843	66,053	262	64,323	181,108	10.1	7.4
Percent change	2000-2010	11.1%	36.3	44.9	30.9	-18.3	21.7	-26.3	61.7	41.7	22.7	27.5
Montana	2010	482,825	73,218	10,082	5,964	2,126	38,510	283	16,253	34,425	15.2	7.1
	2000	412,633	53,966	9,163	5,581	2,540	24,213	248	12,221	29,505	13.1	7.2
Percent change	2000-2010	17.0%	35.7	10.0	6.9	-16.3	59.0	14.1	33.0	16.7	16.0	-0.3
Nebraska	2010	796,793	75,663	24,404	9,167	4,083	13,881	60	24,068	61,722	9.5	7.7
	2000	722,668	56,484	17,936	8,284	4,582	11,912	127	13,643	44,445	7.8	6.2
Percent change	2000-2010	10.3%	34.0	36.1	10.7	-10.9	16.5	-52.8	76.4	38.9	21.5	26.0
Nevada	2010	1,173,814	167,564	61,985	32,949	5,254	32,703	242	34,431	134,619	14.3	11.5
	2000	827,457	76,292	31,635	12,021	4,209	16,526	281	11,620	59,485	9.2	7.2
Percent change	2000-2010	41.9%	119.6	95.9	174.1	24.8	97.9	-13.9	196.3	126.3	54.8	59.5

State	Year	Housing units	Total vacancies	For rent or sale	For sale only	Rented or sold, not occupied	For seasonal, recreational, or occasional use	For migrant workers	Other vacant	Total nonseasonal vacant units	Vacant units' share of housing stock	Nonseasonal vacant units' share of housing stock
New Hampshire	2010	614,754	95,781	13,293	7,521	2,180	63,910	27	8,850	31,844	15.6	5.2
	2000	547,024	72,418	5,218	3,252	1,898	56,413	29	5,608	15,976	13.2	2.9
Percent change	2000-2010	12.4%	32.3	154.8	131.3	14.9	13.3	-6.9	57.8	99.3	17.7	77.4
New Jersey	2010	3,553,562	339,202	92,118	39,260	12,723	134,903	156	60,042	204,143	9.5	5.7
	2000	3,310,275	245,630	49,858	24,546	15,206	109,075	246	46,699	136,309	7.4	4.1
Percent change	2000-2010	7.3%	38.1	84.8	59.9	-16.3	23.7	-36.6	28.6	49.8	28.6	39.5
New Mexico	2010	901,388	109,993	22,150	11,050	3,446	36,612	229	36,506	73,152	12.2	8.1
	2000	780,579	102,608	26,697	10,693	4,738	31,990	332	28,158	70,286	13.1	9.0
Percent change	2000-2010	15.5%	7.2	-17.0	3.3	-27.3	14.4	-31.0	29.6	4.1	-7.2	-9.9
New York	2010	8,108,103	790,348	200,039	77,225	33,813	289,301	892	189,078	500,155	9.7	6.2
	2000	7,679,307	622,447	158,569	59,405	40,439	235,043	750	128,241	386,654	8.1	5.0
Percent change	2000-2010	5.6%	27.0	26.2	30.0	-16.4	23.1	18.9	47.4	29.4	20.3	22.5
North Carolina	2010	4,327,528	582,373	156,587	71,693	21,181	191,508	1,620	139,784	389,245	13.5	9.0
	2000	3,523,944	391,931	92,893	44,007	26,523	134,870	1,890	91,748	255,171	11.1	7.2
Percent change	2000-2010	22.8%	48.6	68.6	62.9	-20.1	42.0	-14.3	52.4	52.5	21.0	24.2
North Dakota	2010	317,498	36,306	7,422	2,734	1,597	11,483	319	12,751	24,504	11.4	7.7
	2000	289,677	32,525	7,642	4,713	1,631	8,340	263	9,936	23,922	11.2	8.3
Percent change	2000-2010	9.6%	11.6	-2.9	-42.0	-2.1	37.7	21.3	28.3	2.4	1.8	-6.5

Table 5. (Continued)

State	Year	Housing units	Total vacancies	For rent or sale	For sale only	Rented or sold, not occupied	For seasonal, recreational, or occasional use	For migrant workers	Other vacant	Total nonseasonal vacant units	Vacant units' share of housing stock	Nonseasonal vacant units' share of housing stock
Ohio	2010	5,127,508	524,073	184,143	78,089	27,389	58,591	346	175,515	465,136	10.2	9.1
	2000	4,783,051	337,278	125,095	48,404	33,182	47,239	355	83,003	289,684	7.1	6.1
Percent change	2000-2010	7.2%	55.4	47.2	61.3	-17.5	24.0	-2.5	111.5	60.6	44.9	49.8
Oklahoma	2010	1,664,378	203,928	59,264	22,671	11,122	35,187	318	75,366	168,423	12.3	10.1
	2000	1,514,400	172,107	50,165	23,725	14,228	32,293	232	51,464	139,582	11.4	9.2
Percent change	2000-2010	9.9%	18.5	18.1	-4.4	-21.8	9.0	37.1	46.4	20.7	7.8	9.8
Oregon	2010	1,675,562	156,624	40,193	24,191	7,009	55,473	461	29,297	100,690	9.3	6.0
	2000	1,452,709	118,986	37,482	20,349	7,158	36,850	333	16,814	81,803	8.2	5.6
Percent change	2000-2010	15.3%	31.6	7.2	18.9	-2.1	50.5	38.4	74.2	23.1	14.1	6.7
Pennsylvania	2010	5,567,315	548,411	135,262	64,818	29,517	161,582	411	156,821	386,418	9.9	6.9
	2000	5,249,750	472,747	105,585	55,891	37,494	148,230	386	125,161	324,131	9.0	6.2
Percent change	2000-2010	6.0%	16.0	28.1	16.0	-21.3	9.0	6.5	25.3	19.2	9.4	12.4
Rhode Island	2010	463,388	49,788	15,763	5,171	1,946	17,077	12	9,819	32,699	10.7	7.1
	2000	439,837	31,413	8,615	2,400	1,726	12,988	14	5,670	18,411	7.1	4.2
Percent change	2000-2010	5.4%	58.5	83.0	115.5	12.7	31.5	-14.3	73.2	77.6	50.4	68.6
South Carolina	2010	2,137,683	336,502	92,758	36,523	12,476	112,531	370	81,844	223,601	15.7	10.5
	2000	1,753,670	219,816	58,176	21,955	15,930	70,198	420	53,137	149,198	12.5	8.5
Percent change	2000-2010	21.9%	53.1	59.4	66.4	-21.7	60.3	-11.9	54.0	49.9	25.6	22.9

State	Year	Housing units	Total vacancies	For rent or sale	For sale only	Rented or sold, not occupied	For seasonal, recreational, or occasional use	For migrant workers	Other vacant	Total nonseasonal vacant units	Vacant units' share of housing stock	Nonseasonal vacant units' share of housing stock
South Dakota	2,010	363,438	41,156	10,366	3,696	1,956	13,277	88	11,773	27,791	11.3	7.6
	2,000	323,208	32,963	8,057	3,718	2,053	9,839	35	9,261	23,089	10.2	7.1
Percent change	2000-2010	12.4%	24.9	28.7	-0.6	-4.7	34.9	151.4	27.1	20.4	11.0	7.0
Tennessee	2,010	2,812,133	318,581	98,370	47,274	14,498	60,778	392	97,269	257,411	11.3	9.2
	2000	2,439,443	206,538	64,476	31,876	14,838	36,712	442	58,194	169,384	8.5	6.9
Percent change	2000-2010	15.3%	54.2	52.6	48.3	-2.3	65.6	-11.3	67.1	52.0	33.8	31.8
Texas	2010	9,977,436	1,054,503	394,310	121,430	46,946	208,733	2,209	280,875	843,561	10.6	8.5
	2000	8,157,575	764,221	249,240	85,732	49,625	173,149	3,453	203,022	587,619	9.4	7.2
Percent change	2000-2010	22.3%	38.0	58.2	41.6	-5.4	20.6	-36.0	38.3	43.6	12.8	17.4
Utah	2010	979,709	102,017	20,176	14,580	4,236	47,978	232	14,815	53,807	10.4	5.5
	2000	768,594	67,313	13,780	10,586	3,333	29,685	138	9,791	37,490	8.8	4.9
Percent change	2000-2010	27.5%	51.6	46.4	37.7	27.1	61.6	68.1	51.3	43.5	18.9	12.6
Vermont	2010	322,539	66,097	5,635	3,598	1,212	50,198	39	5,415	15,860	20.5	4.9
	2000	294,382	53,748	3,084	2,393	1,381	43,060	46	3,784	10,642	18.3	3.6
Percent change	2000-2010	9.6%	23.0	82.7	50.4	-12.2	16.6	-15.2	43.1	49.0	12.2	36.0
Virginia	2010	3,364,939	308,881	82,493	44,881	14,978	80,468	608	85,453	227,805	9.2	6.8
	2000	2,904,192	205,019	47,563	27,407	16,254	54,696	652	58,447	149,671	7.1	5.2
Percent change	2000-2010	15.9%	50.7	73.4	63.8	-7.9	47.1	-6.7	46.2	52.2	30.0	31.4
Washington	2010	2,885,677	265,601	72,112	41,417	12,500	89,907	1,328	48,337	174,366	9.2	6.0

Table 5. (Continued)

State	Year	Housing units	Total vacancies	For rent or sale	For sale only	Rented or sold, not occupied	For seasonal, recreational, or occasional use	For migrant workers	Other vacant	Total nonseasonal vacant units	Vacant units' share of housing stock	Nonseasonal vacant units' share of housing stock
	2000	2,451,075	179,677	50,887	27,255	11,256	60,355	1,197	28,727	118,125	7.3	4.8
Percent change	2000-2010	17.7%	47.8	41.7	52.0	11.1	49.0	10.9	68.3	47.6	25.6	25.4
West Virginia	2010	881,917	118,086	19,521	10,381	5,963	38,283	118	43,820	79,685	13.4	9.0
	2000	844,623	108,142	18,286	12,243	7,954	32,757	61	36,841	75,324	12.8	8.9
Percent change	2000-2010	4.4%	9.2	6.8	-15.2	-25.0	16.9	93.4	18.9	5.8	4.6	1.3
Wisconsin	2010	2,624,358	344,590	63,268	34,219	9,436	193,046	249	44,372	151,295	13.1	5.8
	2000	2,321,144	236,600	38,714	17,172	9,386	142,313	205	28,810	94,082	10.2	4.1
Percent change	2000-2010	13.1%	45.6	63.4	99.3	0.5	35.6	21.5	54.0	60.8	28.8	42.2
Wyoming	2010	261,868	34,989	7,304	3,376	1,239	14,892	322	7,856	19,775	13.4	7.6
	2000	223,854	30,246	6,214	2,977	1,445	12,389	246	6,975	17,611	13.5	7.9
Percent change	2000-2010	17.0%	15.7	17.5	13.4	-14.3	20.2	30.9	12.6	12.3	-1.1	-4.0

Source: Census 2000 and 2010 data.

Table 6 shows the total number of vacant residential units in 2000 and 2010 according to decennial Census data, as well as the percentage change between the two censuses. The table also shows the states ranked by number of residential vacant units in 2010, with Florida at the top because of the large number of vacant units in that state in 2010.

Table 6. Number of Vacant Residential Units, 2010 Census

State	Vacancies 2010	Vacancies 2000	Percent change 2000-2010
United States	14,988,438	10,424,540	43.8
Florida	1,568,778	965,018	62.6
California	1,102,583	711,679	54.9
Texas	1,054,503	764,221	38.0
New York	790,348	622,447	27.0
Michigan	659,725	448,618	47.1
North Carolina	582,373	391,931	48.6
Pennsylvania	548,411	472,747	16.0
Ohio	524,073	337,278	55.4
Georgia	503,217	275,368	82.7
Arizona	463,536	287,862	61.0
Illinois	459,743	293,836	56.5
Wisconsin	344,590	236,600	45.6
New Jersey	339,202	245,630	38.1
Missouri	337,118	247,423	36.3
South Carolina	336,502	219,816	53.1
Tennessee	318,581	206,538	54.2
Virginia	308,881	205,019	50.7
Indiana	293,387	196,013	49.7
Alabama	288,062	226,631	27.1
Washington	265,601	179,677	47.8
Massachusetts	261,179	178,409	46.4
Minnesota	259,974	170,819	52.2
Colorado	240,030	149,799	60.2
Louisiana	236,621	191,128	23.8
Maryland	222,403	164,424	35.3
Kentucky	207,199	160,280	29.3
Oklahoma	203,928	172,107	18.5
Arkansas	169,215	130,347	29.8

Table 6. (Continued)

State	Vacancies 2010	Vacancies 2000	Percent change 2000-2010
Nevada	167,564	76,292	119.6
Maine	164,611	133,701	23.1
Mississippi	158,951	115,519	37.6
Oregon	156,624	118,986	31.6
Kansas	121,119	93,309	29.8
West Virginia	118,086	108,142	9.2
Connecticut	116,804	84,305	38.5
Iowa	114,841	83,235	38.0
New Mexico	109,993	102,608	7.2
Utah	102,017	67,313	51.6
New Hampshire	95,781	72,418	32.3
Idaho	88,388	58,179	51.9
Nebraska	75,663	56,484	34.0
Montana	73,218	53,966	35.7
Vermont	66,097	53,748	23.0
Hawaii	64,170	57,302	12.0
Delaware	63,588	44,336	43.4
Rhode Island	49,788	31,413	58.5
Alaska	48,909	39,378	24.2
South Dakota	41,156	32,963	24.9
North Dakota	36,306	32,525	11.6
Wyoming	34,989	30,246	15.7
District of Columbia	30,012	26,507	13.2

Sources: Census 2000 and 2010 data.

End Notes

[1] In this report, we generally refer to vacant properties as properties with unoccupied structures on them.

[2] The Troubled Asset Relief Program was authorized by the Emergency Economic Stabilization Act of 2008. Pub. L. No. 110-343, 122 Stat. 3765 (2008), codified at 12 U.S.C. §§ 5201 et seq.

[3] The first phase of this program, NSP 1, was authorized by the Housing and Economic Recovery Act of 2008, Pub. L. No. 110-289, 122 Stat. 2654 (2008), which provided $3.92 billion in grant funds. The American Recovery and Reinvestment Act of 2009, Pub. L. No. 111-5, 123 Stat. 115 (2009) provided an additional $2 billion in NSP funds (referred to as NSP 2)

and changed several aspects of the program. Later, the Wall Street Reform and Consumer Protection Act, Pub. L. No. 111-203, 124 Stat. 1376 (2010) (Dodd-Frank Act), provided an additional $1 billion in funding for the program (referred to as NSP 3).

[4] A "holder" "is a person who has legal possession of a negotiable instrument and is entitled to receive payment on it." *Black's Law Dictionary* (9th ed., 2009).

[5] Fannie Mae and Freddie Mac share a primary mission that has been to stabilize and assist the U.S. secondary mortgage market and facilitate the flow of mortgage credit. To accomplish this goal, the enterprises issue debt and stock and use the proceeds to purchase conventional mortgages that meet their underwriting standards, known as conforming mortgages, from primary mortgage lenders such as banks or thrifts. The enterprises hold some of the mortgages that they purchase in their portfolios. However, most of the mortgages are packaged into mortgage-backed securities, which are sold to investors in the secondary mortgage market. In September 2008, FHFA placed Fannie Mae and Freddie Mac into conservatorship out of concern that their deteriorating financial condition threatened the stability of financial markets. 6The FHA single-family mortgage insurance program insures private lenders against losses from borrower defaults on mortgages that meet FHA criteria. To support the program, FHA imposes up-front and annual mortgage insurance premiums on home buyers. Similarly, the Department of Veterans Affairs guaranty program allows mortgage lenders to extend loans to eligible veterans on favorable terms and provides lenders with substantial financial protections against the losses associated with extending such mortgages.

[7] A short sale is a foreclosure alternative where the lender agrees to accept proceeds from the sale of the home to a third party even though the sales prices is less than the principal and accrued interest and other expenses owed.

[8] According to a GSE representative, if a property is still occupied after the foreclosure sale and any redemption period are complete, servicers or entities working on behalf of the GSEs may assess the occupant for a rental program while the property is being marketed for sale or offer relocation assistance payments for the occupant's voluntary cooperation in vacating the property.

[9] 12 U.S.C. § 1813(q).

[10] "Federal consumer financial law" is a defined term in the Dodd-Frank Act that includes over a dozen existing federal consumer protection laws, including the Truth in Lending Act, the Real Estate Settlement Procedures Act, and the Equal Credit Opportunity Act, as well as title X of the Dodd-Frank Act itself. 12 U.S.C. § 5481(12), (14).

[11] Other federal data collection efforts that include vacant property data are the Census/HUD American Housing Survey and the Current Population Survey/Housing Vacancy Survey, but these surveys did not collect the data at the geographic level or at the sample size needed for our study.

[12] See GAO, *2010 Census: Data Collection Operations Were Generally Completed as Planned, but Long-standing Challenges Suggest Need for Fundamental Reforms,* GAO-11-193 (Washington, D.C.: Dec. 14, 2010).

[13] Various entities define the term "vacant" differently. For example, the decennial census defines a vacant housing unit as one in which no one is living on Census Day. The USPS defines a vacant address as an unoccupied address where mail has not been deliverable for 90 days or longer. One nongovernmental organization defined a vacant property as a site that poses a threat to public safety or one that owners neglect. Baltimore city's building code defines "vacant" as "an unoccupied structure that is unsafe or unfit for human habitation or other

authorized use." (Building, Fire, and Related Codes of Baltimore City, Part II, §116.4.1, 2011, as last amended by Ord. 11-419).

[14] Census 2010 and USPS data also do not distinguish between single-family and multifamily residential units.

[15] Census officials also stated that some properties, which the enumerators determined were "uninhabitable," were deleted from the Census data on the national housing stock and were not counted as housing units. As a result, they were not categorized as either occupied or vacant. These properties generally were those that were severely deteriorated and were unlikely ever to be reoccupied, according to Census officials.

[16] Our estimates of nonseasonal vacant units exclude vacant properties for seasonal use or for use by migrant workers because these are occupied for temporary periods of time, and we concluded that such properties are likely to be maintained. The total number of vacant properties in the United States, including all vacant properties identified in the Census data, increased 44 percent between 2000 and 2010, from 10 million to almost 15 million. See appendix II for more details about the Census data.

[17] We compared the estimates from the 2010 Census data with USPS data on counts of vacant addresses by state for the second quarter of 2010. We found that 9 of the 10 states with the largest number of vacant addresses according to the USPS data were also among the 10 states with the largest number of nonseasonal vacant housing units in the 2010 Census data. Various reasons may explain why the USPS and Census data differ somewhat, including that the Census data includes short-term vacant properties that are for rent or for sale, while the USPS data includes only addresses where mail has not been deliverable for 90 days or longer.

[18] Census vacancy data are also available at the level of individual street blocks.

[19] As an additional way to assess the level of economic distress in localities, we analyzed ACS data for the 9 cities we studied for the period 2005 through 2009 (2010 poverty data were not yet available at the time we undertook this analysis) to identify the percentage of households in a given census tract with annual incomes below the appropriate poverty threshold for that household size and composition as defined by the Census Bureau.

[20] GAO, *Mortgage Foreclosures: Additional Mortgage Servicer Actions Could Help Reduce the Frequency and Impact of Abandoned Foreclosures*, GAO-11-93 (Washington, D.C.: Nov. 15, 2010).

[21] This estimate was developed by a local housing research organization using data from the city's database.

[22] To calculate its estimate of vacant, abandoned properties, the department used information including code enforcement orders for boarding up of vacant properties, relevant police and arson reports, undelivered mail, and property and tax information from the county land records.

[23] GAO-11-93.

[24] Woodstock Institute, *Left Behind: Troubled Foreclosed Properties and Servicer Accountability in Chicago* (Chicago, IL, January 2011).

[25] According to HUD, as of July 2008, 25 states used a nonjudicial process as their normal method of foreclosure, 19 states use judicial, and 6 states use both. See GAO-11-93 for more information about these different processes.

[26] *The Post-Foreclosure Experience of U.S. Households*. Raven Molloy and Hui Shan. Federal Reserve Board, Washington, D.C. May 2011.

[27] James H. Carr and Michelle Mulcahey, *Rebuilding Communities in Economic Distress: Local strategies to Sustain Homeownership, Reclaim Vacant Properties, and Promote*

Community-Based Employment. National Community Reinvestment Coalition (Washington, D.C.: October 2010).

[28] GAO-11-433.

[29] Stephan Whitaker, *Economic Commentary: Foreclosure-Related Vacancy Rates.* Federal Reserve Bank of Cleveland, July 26, 2011.

[30] CoreLogic, *U.S. Housing and Mortgage Trends* (February 2011).

[31] As we have previously reported, house price appreciation or depreciation in a geographic area is commonly measured by changes in a house price index. See GAO, *Loan Performance and Negative Home Equity in the Nonprime Mortgage Market,* GAO-10-146R (Washington, D.C.: Dec. 16, 2009).

[32] The two indexes are the FHFA and S&P/Case-Shiller indexes. The FHFA index, which consists of separate indexes for 384 metropolitan areas, is based on sales and appraisal data for properties with mortgages purchased or securitized by Fannie Mae or Freddie Mac (conforming mortgages). To be eligible for purchase by these entities, loans (and borrowers receiving the loans) must meet specified requirements. The S&P/Case-Shiller national index, which is a composite of separate indexes for the nine regional Census divisions, is based on sales data for homes purchased with both conforming and nonconforming mortgages.

[33] Maureen F. Maitland and David M. Blitzer. *S&P/Case-Shiller Home Price Indices 2010, A Year In Review*. January 2011.

[34] Joint Center for Housing Studies, *State of the Nation's Housing, 2011.* Harvard University.

[35] The International Code Council is an association to help the building safety community and construction industry provide safe, sustainable and affordable construction through the development of codes and standards used in the design, build and compliance process. According to the International Code Council, 50 states and the District of Columbia have adopted these codes at the state or jurisdictional level.

[36] Local homeowners' associations also may have their own maintenance standards that property owners must follow and the associations or surrounding residents within a neighborhood sometimes expend resources on maintenance activities such as mowing lawns or removing trash when properties are left unattended.

[37] Securitization trusts have another entity that acts as trustee. Trustees keep records and receive mortgage payments from servicers and disperse them among investors according to the terms of the pooling and servicing agreement. In addition, trustees are the legal owners of record of the mortgage loans on behalf of the trust. Mortgage servicers administer the loans underlying mortgage-backed securities under contractual agreements with the securitization trustee, which acts on behalf of the owners of the securitization trust's securities. Any legal action a servicer takes on behalf of the trust, such as foreclosure, generally may be brought in the name of the trustee.

[38] Certain loans may be required to have private mortgage insurance, which covers a lender for certain losses related to the potential default of the loan. Insurance claims from private mortgage insurers may also include reimbursement to servicers for property maintenance expenses.

[39] According to HUD preservation and protection guidelines, at the time of conveyance to HUD, a property must be undamaged by fire, flood, earthquake, hurricane, tornado, or mortgagee neglect, as set forth in and required by 24 C.F.R. §203.378. For condominiums that were secured by mortgages insured under §234 of the National Housing Act, the property must also be undamaged by boiler explosion, as required by 24 C.F.R. § 234.270. In addition, the property must be secured, the lawn maintained, winterized (as applicable), and interior and

exterior debris must be removed with the property's interior maintained in broom-swept condition. This includes the removal of any vehicles and removal of any personal property in accordance with local and state requirements.

[40] The data from FHA did not specify categories of expenses during the foreclosure period.

[41] These figures may include costs for both vacant and occupied properties. GSE representatives told us that between 50 percent and 60 percent of properties are vacant at the start of the postforeclosure sale period, but by the end of the period all properties are vacant or an REO purchaser has agree to purchase the property while it is occupied.

[42] According to one industry participant's study, pooling and servicing agreements typically direct servicers to manage and dispose of REO properties according to any specific contractual requirements in the agreement, generally accepted servicing practices, and the requirements of local laws and regulations. Stergios Theologides, *Servicing REO Properties: The Servicer's Role and Incentives*, REO & Vacant Properties, Strategies for Neighborhood Stabilization, a joint publication of the Federal Reserve Banks of Boston and Cleveland and the Federal Reserve Board (Sept. 1, 2010).

[43] For example, according to staff from a property maintenance company, certain states may require servicers to obtain a court order before accessing a property in foreclosure or during the redemption period or they would be subject to trespassing.

[44] Representatives of one large servicer told us that as of July 2011, the company changed its policy to continue maintaining such properties in the interest of neighborhood stabilization.

[45] See GAO-11-93. We noted in this report that the vast majority of abandoned foreclosures were loans that involved third-party investors and private label mortgage- backed securities. GSE-purchased loans account for a very small portion of our estimated number of abandoned foreclosures. Similarly, we found only about 0.3 percent of abandoned foreclosures were associated with FHA, VA, or Ginnie Mae insured loans.

[46] Woodstock Institute, *Left Behind*.

[47] GAO-11-93.

[48] GAO-11-93

[49] See, for example, William C. Apgar, Mark Duda, and Rochelle Nawrocki Gorey, *The Municipal Cost of Foreclosures: A Chicago Case Study*, Housing Finance Policy Research Paper 2005-1, Homeownership Preservation Foundation (Minneapolis, Minn.: 2005); Christiana McFarland, Casey Dawkins, and C. Theodore (Ted) Koebel, "Local Housing Conditions and Contexts: A Framework for Policy Making" (Washington: National League of Cities, 2007); and Dan Immergluck and Geoff Smith, "The Impact of Single-family Mortgage Foreclosures on Neighborhood Crime," Housing Studies 21, no. 6 (2006): 851-866.

[50] GAO-11-93.

[51] See, for example, Brian A. Mikelbank, "Spatial Analysis of the Impact of Vacant, Abandoned and Foreclosed Properties," study conducted for the Office of Community Affairs, Federal Reserve Bank of Cleveland, 2008; and Kai-yan Lee, "Foreclosure's Price- Depressing Spillover Effects on Local Properties: A Literature Review," Community Affairs Discussion Paper, Federal Reserve Bank of Boston (Boston: 2008). Each of the studies we reviewed focused on specific geographic locations, so their results cannot be generalized to the state level or the country as a whole. The studies also each also use data from different time periods and use different approaches.

[52] Kai-yan Lee. 53William C. Apgar, Mark Duda, and Rochelle Nawrocki Gorey. 54Stephan Whitaker and Thomas J. Fitzpatrick IV. *The Impact of Vacant, Tax-Delinquent, and*

Foreclosed Property on Sales Prices of Neighboring Homes. Federal Reserve Bank of Cleveland, September 2011.

[55] Brian A. Mikelbank. This study looked at the impact on sales price separating the effect of foreclosed properties and vacant/abandoned properties, and also accounting for neighborhood characteristics that could otherwise have distorted the results. The study also noted that the vacant properties were located close to the center of Columbus, Ohio, whereas the foreclosed properties were distributed more widely across the city.

[56] Nigel G. Griswold and Patricia E. Norris, *Economic Impacts of Residential Property Abandonment and the Genesee County Land Bank in Flint, Michigan.* Report #2007-05, MSU Land Policy Institute, (Lansing, MI: April 2007).

[57] Christopher W. Hoene and Michael A. Pagano, *Research Brief on America's Cities, September 2011.* National League of Cities. The National League of Cities works in a partnership with 49 state municipal leagues and serves as a resource to and an advocate for the more than 19,000 cities, villages, and towns it represents.

[58] The report notes that a downturn in real estate prices may not be noticed for one to several years after an economic downturn began because property tax assessment cycles vary across jurisdictions: some reassess property annually, while others reassess every few years.

[59] See Frank Alexander, "Tax Liens, Tax Sales, and Due Process," *75 Ind. L. J.* 747 (2000). Vacant, abandoned properties with unpaid taxes may go through the jurisdiction's tax foreclosure processes. These processes generally take the form of either property auctions or sales of the outstanding tax liens to private entities. The purchasers of tax liens may not pay property taxes in subsequent years or adequately maintain the property.

[60] GAO-11-93.

[61] GAO-11-93.

[62] Officials in the city of Tucson stated that their revenues depend largely on sales taxes, though sales tax revenue has also declined as a result of the recent poor economic conditions.

[63] Community Research Partners, *$60 Million and Counting: The cost of vacant and abandoned properties to eight Ohio cities* (Columbus, OH: Feb. 2008). The study reviewed the magnitude and cost of vacant and abandoned properties in eight Ohio cities—Cleveland, Columbus, Dayton, Ironton, Lima, Springfield, Toledo, and Zanesville— and found $49 million in cumulative lost property tax revenues to these local governments and school districts.

[64] GAO-10-146R.

[65] While not a focus of this report, most of these localities are also engaged in foreclosure mitigation and prevention strategies.

[66] Enterprise Community Partners, Inc., *Market Data-Driven Stabilization: A Case Study of Cleveland's NEO CANDO Data System* (Washington, D.C.: 2010).

[67] The Trust is a national nonprofit organization formed in 2008 by four national organizations in the housing and community development field—Enterprise Community Partners, Housing Partnership Network, Local Initiatives Support Corporation, and NeighborWorks America. These four founding organizations were soon joined by the National Urban League and the National Council of La Raza as prominent sponsors of the Trust.

[68] Daniel Fleischman, *Nonprofit Strategies for Returning REO Properties to Effective Use*, REO & Vacant Properties, Strategies for Neighborhood Stabilization, a joint publication of the Federal Reserve Banks of Boston and Cleveland and the Federal Reserve Board (Sept. 1, 2010).

[69] In a recent speech, Elizabeth Duke, Member of the Board of Governors of the Federal Reserve System noted that, in some cases, properties are too damaged, or otherwise too low-value,

to be sold as owner-occupied units or profitably converted to rental properties. She said that the Federal Reserve estimates about 5 percent of properties in the REO inventory of FHA and the GSEs are valued at less than $20,000. See *Federal Reserve Board Policy Forum: The Housing Market Going Forward, Lessons Learned from the Recent Crisis* (Washington, D.C.: Sept. 1, 2011).

[70] Specifically, the study estimated that property values increased between $117 and $50,000 per property. Nigel G. Griswold and Patricia E. Norris.

[71] Stephan Whitaker and Thomas J. Fitzpatrick IV.

[72] The specific order in which liens must be paid in the event of foreclosure or sale varies depending on the jurisdiction.

[73] GAO-11-93.

[74] Chicago, Ill, Municipal Code § 13-12-125, 135.

[75] *See* N.J. Stat. Ann. § 46:10B-51 (2010). The New Jersey requirements were included in the Mortgage Stabilization and Relief Act, 2008 N.J. Sess. Law Serv. Ch. 127 (West) and amended by the New Jersey Foreclosure Fairness Act, 2009 N.J. Sess. Law Serv. Ch. 296 (West). *See* N.Y. Real Prop. Law § 1307 (2010). The New York requirements were effective April 14, 2010.

[76] Colo. Rev. Stat. § 38-38-901, et seq., which was effective as of August 1, 2010, authorizes an expedited foreclosure sale procedure if the mortgagee can document that the property is abandoned (vacant). A signed affidavit that is based upon the personal knowledge of the noteholder, their agent, the sheriff of the county in which the property is located, or a building inspector, or other municipal or county official having jurisdiction over the property is prima facie evidence of abandonment. The affidavit should state that the property is not actually occupied and that the signer has inspected the property more than once and each time determined that the property is abandoned and that at least two of the following facts exist: (1) windows or entrances to the property are boarded up or closed off, or multiple window panes are broken and unrepaired; (2) doors to the property are smashed through, broken off, unhinged or continuously unlocked; (3) gas, electric, and water service to the property have been terminated for a period of at least 30 days; (4) the police or sheriff's office has received at least two reports of trespassers on the property, or of vandalism or other illegal acts being committed on the property; or (5) the property is deteriorating and is either below or is in imminent danger of falling below minimum local government standards for public safety and sanitation. The affidavit must also be accompanied by photographic or other documentary evidence such as police reports demonstrating of the cited conditions. The procedure is not applicable to judicial foreclosures.

[77] The judge we spoke with in Chicago told us that the city established the housing court under its home rule authority granted to it by the state of Illinois.

[78] The results of the model are not the only factor determining whether a borrower will receive a loan modification. For example, borrowers might not be interested in a loan modification, even if approved.

[79] Bob Winthrop and Rebecca Herr, *Determining the Cost of Vacancies in Baltimore*, Government Finance Review (June 2009).

[80] Alan Mallach, *REO Properties, Housing Markets, and the Shadow Inventory*, REO and Vacant Properties, Strategies for Neighborhood Stabilization, a joint publication of the Federal Reserve Banks of Boston and Cleveland and the Federal Reserve Board (Sept. 1, 2010).

[81] The HAMP decision-making model—called the net present value (NPV) model—was developed by an interagency working group made up of officials from FDIC, Fannie Mae,

Freddie Mac, FHFA, and Treasury. Servicers participating in HAMP use this model to decide whether to modify a loan. Servicers with at least a $40 billion servicing book may customize the NPV model for use in HAMP, but they must use standard model inputs for certain variables. Some servicers have also developed their own models to analyze borrowers' eligibility for their own proprietary modification programs if they are not eligible for HAMP. They told us that their proprietary models generally used similar inputs as the HAMP NPV model.

[82] As outlined in the March 4, 2009, program guidelines, HAMP's eligibility requirements stipulate that (1) the property must be owner-occupied and the borrower's primary residence (the program excludes vacant and investor-owned properties); (2) the property must be a single-family (1-4 unit) property with a maximum unpaid principal balance on the unmodified first-lien mortgage that is equal to or less than $729,750 for a 1-unit property; (3) the loans must have been originated on or before January 1, 2009; and (4) the first-lien mortgage payment must be more than 31 percent of the homeowner's gross monthly income.

[83] A HUD official explained how the agency's technical assistance has helped local officials analyze their local markets and adjust their strategies for spending NSP funds on programs that would be most effective. HUD has recently revised its NSP technical assistance efforts to better target spending to communities that need it the most and has developed Web-based resources for all NSP grantees. HUD also plans to launch a similar strategy for its other grant programs that is aimed at improving the capacity of local governments, especially in economically distressed cities.

[84] Pub. L. No. 111- 5, 123 Stat. 115 (2009).

[85] GAO, *Troubled Asset Relief Program: Treasury Actions Needed to Make the Home Affordable Modification Program More Transparent and Accountable,* GAO-09-837 (Washington, D.C.: July 23, 2009). Treasury has begun implementing several other programs for struggling homeowners, including the Second-Lien Modification Program, the Principal Reduction Alternative program for borrowers who owe more on their mortgages than the value of their homes, and the Home Affordable Foreclosure Alternatives program for those who are not successful in HAMP modifications. However, we reported that Treasury's progress in implementing these programs has been slow. See *Troubled Asset Relief Program: Treasury Continues to Face Implementation Challenges and Data Weaknesses in Its Making Home Affordable Program*, GAO-11-288 (Washington, D.C.: Mar. 17, 2011). As of July 2011, Treasury reported that there were 9,221 active Principal Reduction Alternative permanent modifications. See Making Home Affordable, Program Performance Report Through July 2011 found at http://www.treasury.gov/ initiatives/ financial-stability/results/MHA- Reports/Pages/default.aspx.

[86] Section 304 of the Federal Deposit Insurance Corporation Improvement Act of 1991 requires the federal banking agencies to prescribe uniform real estate lending standards. 12 U.S.C. § 1828(o). The standards established by the federal banking regulators require every depository institution to establish and maintain comprehensive, written real estate lending policies that are consistent with safe and sound banking practices and appropriate to the size of the institution and nature and scope of its operations. The lending policies must establish loan portfolio diversification standards; prudent underwriting standards; loan administration procedures for the bank's real estate portfolio; and documentation, approval, and reporting requirements to monitor compliance with the bank's real estate lending policies. OCC (12 C.F.R. Part 34, subpart D), Federal Reserve (12 C.F.R. Part 208, subpart E), FDIC (12 C.F.R. Part 365).

[87] Section 39 of the Federal Deposit Insurance Act (12 U.S.C. 1831p—1) requires that each bank regulator establish certain safety and soundness standards by regulation or guideline. For the OCC, these regulations appear at 12 C.F.R. Part 30; for the Federal Reserve, these regulations appear at 12 C.F.R. 208.3(d)(1); for FDIC, these regulations appear at 12 C.F.R. Part 364, Appendix A.

[88] Because mortgage servicers generally manage loans that are actually owned or held by other entities, they are not exposed to significant losses if the loans become delinquent. In addition, we have previously reported that the percentage of loans in foreclosure was historically very low (less than 1 percent) from 1979 to 2006.

[89] 12 U.S.C. § 29; 12 C.F.R. § 34.82(a). According to regulatory officials, various state laws that apply to certain institutions may have longer or shorter limits on holding REO properties.

[90] Beginning in September 2010, several servicers announced that they were halting or reviewing their foreclosure proceedings throughout the country after allegations that the documents accompanying judicial foreclosures may have been inappropriately signed or notarized. For more information about this issue, see GAO, *Mortgage Foreclosures: Documentation Problems Reveal Need for Ongoing Regulatory Oversight,* GAO-11-433 (Washington, D.C.: May 2, 2011).

[91] GAO-11-433.

[92] According to a GSE representative, the GSEs are required to establish appropriate incentives to encourage and support servicer contact with borrowers in the early stages of delinquency, consistent timelines and requirements for communications with borrowers, incentive structures for early engagement, and updated foreclosure process timelines. The representative also noted that the work will include consideration of appropriate penalties to encourage efficient resolution and liquidation of properties in cases where foreclosure is necessary.

[93] For example, analysts at Credit Suisse estimate that reducing Fannie Mae's and Freddie Mac's foreclosed-property sales to around 30,000 each month, from the current rate of 50,000, would cut total distressed sales and avoid a further 3 percent to 5 percent decline in home prices. In addition, according to an analyst with Zelman & Associates, an industry research and analysis firm, the number of single-family rental households has increased nationwide in the last several years, especially in markets hard-hit by foreclosures.

[94] GAO, *Troubled Asset Relief Program: Home Affordable Modification Program Continues to Face Implementation Challenges*, GAO-10-556T (Washington, D.C.: Mar. 25, 2010). We also have ongoing work reviewing Treasury's recent steps regarding assessing servicers' program performance.

[95] GAO-10-556T.

End Notes for Appendx I

[1] GAO-11-93 and GAO-11-193.

[2] GAO-11-433.

[3] The Census American Community Survey (ACS) is a survey of 3 million households that takes place throughout the year that includes information on residential housing vacancies and poverty, among other data. The ACS data are reported on an annual basis and are also aggregated into 3-year and 5-year datasets.

In: No One Home ISBN: 978-1-61942-829-4
Editors: M. L. Jackson and G. A. White

Chapter 2

HOUSING MARKET DEVELOPMENTS AND THEIR EFFECTS ON LOW- AND MODERATE-INCOME NEIGHBORHOODS

REMARKS BY JANET L. YELLEN VICE CHAIR BOARD OF GOVERNORS OF THE FEDERAL RESERVE SYSTEM AT THE 2011 FEDERAL RESERVE BANK OF CLEVELAND POLICY SUMMIT CLEVELAND, OHIO*

June 9, 2011

Good morning. I very much appreciate your invitation to speak today. The theme of this ninth annual Federal Reserve Bank of Cleveland Policy Summit, "Housing, Human Capital, and Inequality," could not be timelier. Almost no community in America has escaped the effects of the economic downturn, but many low- and moderate-income communities were hit especially hard,

* This is an edited, reformatted and augmented version of Remarks By Janet L. Yellen Vice Chair Board of Governors of the Federal Reserve System at the 2011 Federal Reserve Bank of Cleveland Policy Summit, on June 9, 2011.

including a large number in and around our host city of Cleveland. As one sobering example, almost 10 percent of current Cleveland residents who have ever taken out a mortgage have a foreclosure reflected on their credit report--a rate double that of the rest of the nation.[1]

I will focus today on the state of the housing market and emphasize developments pertaining to low- and moderate-income neighborhoods. I will then discuss policy initiatives to address some of the challenges confronting the housing market.

THE STATE OF THE HOUSING MARKET

As you know, house prices are a critical element in understanding the state of the housing market. Nationally, house prices have been falling for six years, and most industry analysts expect further declines before prices bottom out. Households are equally pessimistic about the trajectory of house prices. According to one prominent survey, only 15 percent of homeowners expect house prices to increase over the next year, and barely half expect house price increases over the next five years.[2]

Largely because of the fall in house prices and the sustained high rate of unemployment, about 4-1/2 percent of mortgages in the United States are currently in foreclosure, and three or more payments have been missed on an additional 3-1/2 percent. In total, 2-1/2 million foreclosures were initiated in 2010, and a similar number of foreclosure starts are expected in 2011.

One factor depressing house prices is the large number of "distressed" home sales. A distressed sale occurs when a borrower sells a house through a short sale or when a lender sells a property that it acquired through a foreclosure; these sales have represented about half of all home sales in recent months. The condition of the property can deteriorate considerably over the course of the foreclosure proceedings, and these damaged properties are typically sold to the next buyer at a significant discount. Commonly, market values of properties and the selling price of similar homes in the neighborhood become depressed as a consequence. The blight associated with these properties can further depress the value of nearby homes.

Housing market conditions are also being hurt by the large inventory of empty and unsold homes in the United States. Nearly 2 million homes were estimated to be vacant in the first quarter of 2011. Although this number is down some from the highs seen in 2008, it is about 60 percent higher than the average level over the 20 years before the 2008 surge. And, with the pipeline of delinquent and foreclosed homes overflowing, the inventory of empty and unsold homes will likely stay elevated for some time, which will maintain downward pressure on house prices and damp construction of new homes.

Recovery in the housing market is being restrained further by tight mortgage credit. According to the Federal Reserve's April 2011 Senior Loan Officer Opinion Survey on Bank Lending Practices, commercial banks have begun to ease standards on credit card and other consumer loans, but they have not yet started to ease standards for residential mortgages, even for those extended to borrowers in the prime market.[3] One sign of this tight credit is the higher credit scores on recent mortgage originations. For example, the median credit score on a prime mortgage originated to purchase a home rose from around 740 in the 2005-07 period to around 780 since mid-2010. Part of this rise may reflect borrower characteristics--perhaps demand for housing has fallen more among borrowers with lower credit scores--but tighter terms and standards undoubtedly play a significant role. These tight standards indicate that some households that might like to purchase a home simply can't obtain the credit to do so.

Under these circumstances, it's not surprising that the demand for housing remains weak. Builders of new homes overwhelmingly report "low to very low" traffic of prospective buyers, as well as expectations of "poor" sales in the months ahead. Similarly, about one-third of the respondents to the Senior Loan Officer Opinion Survey noted weaker demand for mortgages in the first quarter of 2011. Demand is low, in part, because households remain uncertain about the durability of the economic recovery and therefore do not want to commit to such a large investment--especially an investment that may decline further in price.

Although economists may disagree about which of these factors is playing the largest role in the ongoing fall in house prices, all agree that the collapse has left deep scars on many American families and their financial well-being. The drop in house prices is a major factor in the sharp declines in household net worth during the recession. Newly released data from the Federal Reserve Board's 2007-09 Survey of Consumer Finances panel, for example, indicate that the typical homeowner saw a drop in his or her real net worth of about 19 percent over the 2007-09 period. For some homeowners, the loss in net worth was much larger; indeed, nearly one-fourth of homeowners saw their net worth drop by 50 percent or more.[4]

House prices have continued to decline, on net, since 2009, and at this time, more than one-fourth of mortgage borrowers are underwater--that is, have mortgage balances that exceed the current values of their homes. Because of their negative equity stake, many households cannot take advantage of lower interest rates by refinancing their mortgages, nor can they easily sell their homes to pursue better job opportunities elsewhere. In addition, borrowers who are underwater--especially those who also experience a job loss or a cut in work hours or wages--are more likely to default on their mortgages and possibly face foreclosure.

One consequence of the weak demand for housing and the sky-high rate of foreclosures has been a significant drop in the homeownership rate. After fluctuating in a fairly narrow range around 64 percent for nearly three decades, the homeownership rate rose significantly between 1994 and 2004, reaching a peak of 69 percent. Since then, however, the homeownership rate has retraced about half of its earlier increase as many former homeowners have moved into rental housing or made other living arrangements, such as moving in with family members.

Are there any bright spots in this gloomy picture? As the macroeconomy has begun to improve, albeit at an uneven rate, the share of homeowners becoming newly delinquent on their mortgages--that is, missing a payment for the first time—has decreased. In addition, low interest rates and lower house prices have made homeownership potentially more affordable. In fact, by one measure, housing is hovering around its most affordable level in the 22-year history of the series.[5] Of course, tight credit standards have precluded many households from taking advantage of the affordable conditions. Over time, however, as the economy continues to grow and credit conditions improve, more households should be able to benefit from the greater affordability.

THE HOUSING MARKET IN LOW- AND MODERATE-INCOME COMMUNITIES

As I indicated earlier--and as many of you already know--these sobering national trends have had even more devastating effects in low- and moderate-income neighborhoods. To investigate this issue further, researchers at the Federal Reserve classified neighborhoods into three broad categories: low and moderate income, middle income, and high income.[6] A comparison of housing and mortgage market conditions in low- and moderate-income neighborhoods with conditions in high-income neighborhoods reveals several interesting facts.[7]

One notable fact is that house prices in low- and moderate-income neighborhoods rose more than in other neighborhoods during the national boom in house prices, and subsequently fell more during the bust. For example, from 1998 through 2006, house prices, as measured by the CoreLogic repeat-sales house price index, rose 11 percent per year on average in low- and moderate-income neighborhoods, compared with 9 percent per year in high-income neighborhoods. Likewise, during the bust from 2007 to 2010, house prices fell 8 percent per year in lower-income neighborhoods, compared with 7 percent per year in high-income neighborhoods. House price changes also varied more across lower-income neighborhoods than high-income neighborhoods, implying that a greater share of lower-income neighborhoods exhibited price swings that were more dramatic than the overall average.

Linked inextricably to the volatility in house prices in these communities was the volatility of mortgage lending. Mortgage lending surged in low- and moderate-income neighborhoods during the housing boom, and subsequently contracted sharply. Over 2003 to 2006, purchase mortgage originations increased 60 percent in low- and moderate-income neighborhoods but less than 20 percent in high-income neighborhoods. 8 Unfortunately, during this surge in lending many borrowers were encouraged to take out subprime mortgages with teaser rates and prepayment penalties as well as alt-A mortgages with negative amortization features. When these markets collapsed, precipitating an overall tightening in credit conditions, mortgage originations through 2009 fell by 65 percent in low- and moderate-income neighborhoods and 50 percent in high-income neighborhoods.

The greater decline in house prices in low- and moderate-income neighborhoods has had several unfortunate consequences for mortgage borrowers. As of March 2011, borrowers with prime mortgages who lived in these neighborhoods were twice as likely to be underwater as borrowers with prime mortgages in high-income neighborhoods. Because houses are, on average, a much larger share of assets for homeowners in low- and moderate-income neighborhoods, these homeowners had few other assets to draw upon to compensate for the drop in house prices.[9] As a result, borrowers in these neighborhoods who suffered a job loss or other economic misfortune were more likely to default on their mortgages. Indeed, 13 percent of mortgages originated to borrowers in low- and moderate-income neighborhoods were 90 days or more overdue in the first quarter of 2011, compared with 6 percent of mortgages originated to borrowers in high-income neighborhoods.

The higher rates of delinquency suggest that homeownership may have been a riskier proposition over the past decade for households in low- and moderate-income neighborhoods than in high-income neighborhoods. Delinquency rates are higher, in part, because borrowers in these communities were more likely to end up in complicated or inappropriate mortgage products, unacceptably often as a result of unfair and deceptive lending practices. But borrowers in these communities may also be more sensitive to house price declines because they may have fewer financial resources outside of housing, and they may have had little equity in the property to begin with.[10]

Although investing in a home has risks, it also has positive qualities. Households may feel more comfortable investing in housing than in other investments because houses are familiar, tangible, and provide concrete ties to the community. Regular mortgage payments may serve as a useful savings commitment device. Finally, homes pay out a "dividend" in the form of housing services--that is, providing a place to live. The housing services provided by an owner-occupied home--such as control over one's own space--may be preferable to those provided by a rental.

In making a decision about homeownership, prospective buyers need to consider the risks as well as the benefits--in particular, the possibility that house prices can fall and that such declines can have long-lasting effects on their financial well-being. The current decline in national house prices and the preceding run-up were, of course, unusually large even by historical standards. But even during times when house prices were rising nationally, prices fell steeply in certain local markets, such as Texas in the mid-1980s or Massachusetts in the early 1990s. And homeowners are not alone in their difficulty in predicting house prices: The record of industry analysts and economists is also mixed. Although many professionals understood that house values were high at the peak of the recent cycle--probably unsustainably so--there was no consensus about the extent or severity of the coming fall.[11]

In light of this experience, it makes sense to think about the development of wealth-building vehicles for low- and moderate-income households that have some of the desirable qualities of homeownership as an investment, but perhaps have less of the risk. Such instruments should be simple and transparent and might include a savings commitment component. Although households will likely need to take on some risk in order to accumulate wealth, the risk should not have the potential to destroy a household's financial security. Continued research in this area is badly needed.

LOOKING FORWARD

Looking forward, I unfortunately can envision no quick or easy solutions for the problems still afflicting the housing market. Even once it begins to take hold, recovery in the housing market likely will be a long, drawn-out process. For its part, the Federal Reserve will continue to use its policy tools to support the economic recovery and carry out its dual mandate to foster maximum employment in the context of price stability. As the economic recovery progresses and potential homebuyers become more confident about the durability of the recovery, it seems probable that more families will be willing to enter the housing market.

The other factors weighing on the housing market--the high share of distressed sales, the large inventory of vacant homes, and tight mortgage credit--are not affected as directly by macroeconomic policy. Alleviating these conditions will require a different set of responses. Next I will discuss some Federal Reserve initiatives in these areas, and highlight areas in which work still remains to be done.

The high share of distressed sales and the large inventory of vacant homes stem, in large part, from the elevated levels of foreclosures. Federal Reserve officials have stated time and again over the past several years that we believe that lenders and servicers should work actively with troubled borrowers to pursue mortgage modifications whenever possible. The consequences of not conducting modifications are simply too high--for borrowers, for lenders, for the local communities, and for the overall economy.

In the event that a borrower in default no longer wishes to remain in the home, we have urged lenders to make every effort to pursue alternatives to foreclosure, such as short sales or deeds-in-lieu of foreclosure.[12] These alternatives may help the borrower transition to a better housing situation as quickly and seamlessly as possible. In addition, these alternatives may shorten the length of time that a property lies vacant. The deterioration of a property while it lies vacant not only reduces the market value of the property, but also imposes considerable costs on the surrounding community by depressing the prices of neighboring homes, attracting crime, and creating financial burdens for local governments.

The effects of vacant homes on local communities are an example of what economists call a negative externality--that is, an action taken by one party that imposes an uncompensated burden on another. In this case, the externality occurs because lenders, investors, and servicers typically do not bear the burdens resulting from the negative effects of foreclosures on neighborhood house prices, crime, and government budgets. As a result, fewer short sales likely occur than would be best for communities overall. This externality is one of the reasons why a government program that provides financial incentives to servicers and borrowers for pursuing short sales or deeds-in-lieu of foreclosure remains undersubscribed.[13] Indeed, as of March 2011, only about 12,000 agreements had been initiated under the program. This is an area where lenders can and certainly should do more.

The Federal Reserve, in conjunction with other financial banking regulators and government agencies, has embarked on initiatives to help resolve the existing stock of vacant properties and prevent even more properties from entering foreclosure.[14] The first initiative involves revisions to the rules governing the Community Reinvestment Act (CRA) that took effect in January. Under the revised rules, depository institutions receive positive consideration in CRA examinations for participating in community stabilization activities in areas designated as eligible for funds under the Neighborhood Stabilization Program authorized by the Congress. Such activities might include donating properties that they've taken possession of--known as real estate owned--to nonprofit housing organizations or providing financing for the purchase and rehabilitation of foreclosed, abandoned, or vacant properties. Although it is too early to assess the effect of these CRA changes, the participation of more than 600 banks and industry stakeholders in a webinar recently hosted by the Federal Reserve indicates that there is interest and potential in this tool. Our host today, the Federal Reserve Bank of Cleveland, played a key role in envisioning these changes to the CRA rules.

The second initiative, which is ongoing, is the development of uniform national servicing standards. These standards should address the proper handling of both performing and non-performing loans, including loss-mitigation procedures and foreclosure processing, and should lead to improved customer treatment and better transparency and oversight of mortgage servicers' processes. The intent is for servicers to be held to the same standards regardless of their regulator and regardless of whether the loans being serviced are held on the originator's books, have been sold, or have been securitized. By having a common set of standards for the mortgage servicing industry, the financial regulatory agencies will emphasize the importance of servicing practices that promote the best interests of borrowers and the broader housing market.

Let me turn finally to mortgage credit. No one wants to see a return to the loose lending standards that prevailed in the run-up to the crisis, but households and the economy will benefit if we can foster sustainable homeownership with an increase in responsible lending. The Federal Reserve, in coordination with other agencies, has recently published two notices of proposed rulemaking that will affect the provision of mortgage credit. I will describe these rules and explain how we are attempting to balance the objectives of better underwriting and access to credit in the rulemaking process. I should note that both rulemakings are open for comment, and we very much welcome your feedback.

The first set of rules implements the risk-retention provisions of the Dodd-Frank Wall Street Reform and Consumer Protection Act. Broadly speaking, these provisions require issuers of all types of asset-backed securities, including mortgage-backed securities, to retain 5 percent of the credit risk of the assets they securitize.[15] In the runup to the financial crisis, a disproportionate share of mortgage loans was made by lenders who funded their originations through securitizations and effectively retained none of the risk. These lenders had little financial stake in whether the borrowers ultimately repaid the mortgages--sometimes known as having skin in the game--and thus had a reduced incentive to engage in careful underwriting.

The proposed rules outline a flexible menu of ways that securitizers can meet the risk-retention requirement. The proposed rules also have provisions that affect the mortgage market in particular. The rules recognize that the guarantees provided by Fannie Mae and Freddie Mac lead them to retain 100 percent of the credit risk of the mortgages they securitize, and because this guarantee is currently backed by financial support from the government, the proposed rules do not require these government-sponsored enterprises to retain additional risk. Further, as required by the Dodd-Frank Act, the proposed rules exempt securitizations backed entirely by very high-quality mortgages--so-called qualified residential mortgages (QRMs)--from risk retention. The act directed the regulators with rulemaking authority to define QRMs taking into account "underwriting and product features that historical loan performance data indicate result in a lower risk of default." To define QRMs, regulators conducted extensive research on the types of mortgages that have low credit risk, even in stressful economic environments. Under the proposed definition, a qualified residential mortgage must be a closed-end, first-lien mortgage to purchase or refinance a one- to four-family property. Mortgage features cannot include negative amortization, interest-only payments, or the potential for large interest rate increases. Debt-to-income ratios must be conservative, and the borrower's credit history must be relatively clean. Finally, the maximum loan-to-value ratio is 80 percent for purchase mortgages, with no junior lien at closing; 75 percent on rate and term refinance loans; and 70 percent on cash-out refinance loans.

We know that some have expressed anxiety that this narrow definition will result in many borrowers paying higher mortgage rates or being excluded from the credit markets. However, with many creditworthy mortgages not qualifying under the QRM standards, deep funding markets for these products are more likely to develop. As a consequence, we expect that the price difference between mortgages that do and do not qualify under the QRM standard will be relatively small.

Another recently proposed set of rules seeks to ensure that, from now on, all mortgages meet higher underwriting standards, regardless of whether the mortgages are sold into securitizations or retained by lenders on their balance sheets. The QRM standards must also be at least as conservative as these universal higher standards. These revisions to the regulations implementing the Truth in Lending Act are also required by the Dodd-Frank Act. The proposed rules, which were released by the Board in April, establish expanded "ability to repay" requirements for most consumer credit transactions secured by a dwelling. These rules will be finalized by the Consumer Financial Protection Bureau, the new independent agency created by the act.

I know that we are approaching the end of this session, and I fear that my recital of the woes of the housing market may have prevented you from fully enjoying your lunch. So let me close with a reminder that although the problems in the housing market are challenging, many individuals and groups are making a difference, including several pioneering community groups here in Cleveland. We in the Federal Reserve System are pleased to support these efforts by providing data, research, and support, including facilitating important conferences and conversations like the one here today. Thank you very much for your attention. I look forward to answering any questions you might have.

End Notes

[1] I am indebted to Federal Reserve Board staff members Karen Pence and Larry Slifman for their assistance in preparing these remarks. These remarks reflect my own views and not necessarily those of others in the Federal Reserve System.

[2] See Thomson Reuters/University of Michigan Surveys of Consumers.

[3] See the Senior Loan Officer Opinion Survey on Bank Lending Practices; data are available on the Board's website at www.federalreserve.gov/boarddocs/SnLoanSurvey.

[4] For more findings from the 2007-09 Survey of Consumer Finances panel, see Jesse Bricker Brian Bucks, Arthur Kennickell, Traci Mach, and Kevin Moore (2011), "Surveying the Aftermath of the Storm: Changes in Family Finances from 2007 to 2009," Finance and Economics Discussion Series 2011-17 (Washington: Board of Governors of the Federal Reserve System, March), www.federalreserve.gov/pubs/feds/2011/201117/201117abs.html.

[5] See National Association of Realtors (2011), "Affordable Housing Real Estate Resource: Housing Affordability Index," National Association of Realtors, www.realtor.org/research/research/housinginx.

[6] Zip codes and census tracts were classified by whether median household income in that Zip code or census tract was below 80 percent of the median in its metropolitan statistical area, 80 to 120 percent of the median, or more than 120 percent of the median. These income thresholds are used under the Community Reinvestment Act to identify neighborhoods as low and moderate, middle, or high income. Under this scheme, a neighborhood is low income relative to other neighborhoods in its own metropolitan statistical area.

[7] As might be expected, conditions in middle-income neighborhoods lie between the low- and moderateincome and high-income neighborhoods.

[8] For a further discussion of the increase in lending over this period, see, Christopher Mayer, and Karen Pence (2008), "Subprime Mortgages: What, Where, and to Whom?" Finance and Economics Discussion Series 2008-29 (Washington: Board of Governors of the Federal Reserve System, June),.www.federalreserve.gov/pubs/feds/2008/200829/200829abs.html.

[9] Houses represented nearly three-fourths of total assets for homeowners in low- and moderate-income neighborhoods in 2007, according to the Survey of Consumer Finances. In contrast, homes typically represented a bit over half of gross assets for homeowners in higher income neighborhoods in 2007.

[10] The median combined loan-to-value ratio on securitized subprime purchase mortgages originated in 2005 through 2007 was 100 percent. See Christopher Mayer, Karen Pence, and Shane M. Sherlund (2008), "The Rise in Mortgage Defaults," *Journal of Economic Perspectives*, vol. 23(1), pp. 27-50, also available at www.federalreserve.gov /pubs/feds/2008/200859/200859abs.html. For an example of the relationship between house prices and homeownership outcomes, see Kristopher Gerardi, Adam Shapiro, and Paul Willen (2007), "Subprime Outcomes: Risky Mortgages, Homeownership Experiences, and Foreclosures," Working Paper 2007-15 (Boston: Federal Reserve Bank of Boston), www.bos.frb.org/economic/wp/wp2007/wp0715.htm.

[11] For examples, see Kristopher Gerardi, Andreas Lehnert, Shane M. Sherlund, and Paul S. Willen (2008), "Making Sense of the Subprime Crisis," *Brookings Papers on Economic Activity* (Washington: Brookings Institution Press, Fall), pp. 69-145, also available at www.bos.frb.org/economic/ppdp/2009/ppdp0901.htm; and Kristopher S. Gerardi, Christopher L. Foote, and Paul S. Willen (2010), "Reasonable People Did Disagree: Optimism and Pessimism about the U.S. Housing Market before the Crash," Public Policy Discussion Paper 10-5 (Boston: Federal Reserve Bank of Boston, September), www.bos.frb.org/economic/ppdp/2010/ppdp1005.htm.

[12] In a deed-in-lieu of foreclosure, the borrower voluntarily deeds the home to the lender in exchange for being released from the mortgage obligations.

[13] The program is the Home Affordable Foreclosures Alternatives component of the Making Home Affordable program.

[14] The other financial bank regulators for the revised Community Reinvestment Act rules are the Office of the Comptroller of the Currency, the Office of Thrift Supervision, and the Federal Deposit Insurance Corporation. The other financial bank regulators and government

agencies for the national servicing standards are the Office of the Comptroller of the Currency, the Office of Thrift Supervision, the Federal Deposit Insurance Corporation, the Federal Housing Finance Administration, the Department of Housing and Urban Development, and the Department of the Treasury.

[15] The proposed rules were issued jointly. See Office of the Comptroller of the Currency, Board of Governors of the Federal Reserve System, Federal Deposit Insurance Corporation, Federal Housing Finance Agency, Securities and Exchange Commission, and Department of Housing and Urban Development (2011), "Credit Risk Retention; Proposed Rule," (Docket No. 2011-1411), *Federal Register*, vol. 76 (April 29), p. 24090.

In: No One Home ISBN: 978-1-61942-829-4
Editors: M. L. Jackson and G. A. White

Chapter 3

REBALANCING THE HOUSING MARKET

REMARKS BY ELIZABETH A. DUKE MEMBER BOARD OF GOVERNORS OF THE FEDERAL RESERVE SYSTEM AT THE FEDERAL RESERVE BOARD POLICY FORUM: "THE HOUSING MARKET GOING FORWARD: LESSONS LEARNED FROM THE RECENT CRISIS" WASHINGTON, D.C.*

September 1, 2011

Good afternoon. I'd like to join my colleagues in welcoming you to the Federal Reserve Board. This policy forum, "The Housing Market Going Forward: Lessons Learned from the Recent Crisis," has been designed to connect lessons learned from the recent past with policy alternatives that may affect the market for years to come. Determining the key lessons and getting this connection right are important, and as you have already heard, perhaps not

* This is an edited, reformatted and augmented version of Remarks by Elizabeth A. Duke Member Board of Governors of the Federal Reserve System at the Federal Reserve Board Policy Forum: "The Housing Market Going Forward: Lessons Learned from the Recent Crisis", on Septmber 1, 2011.

as easy as it might sound. I would like to offer some suggestions that I think could help. Before I begin, though, I should clarify that the ideas I will be discussing do not necessarily reflect the opinions of my colleagues on the Federal Reserve Board and that these suggestions should not be construed as policy of the Board or the Federal Open Market Committee.

There are many interpretations of the key factors that led to the current state of affairs, and there are a similar number of visions of what the future should look like. But, while it is important to learn from and avoid the mistakes of the recent past, we should not forget what did work for many years in the housing and housing finance markets. So, in crafting appropriate policy responses, an important starting point is to carefully analyze what we're solving for. Certainly we want a solution based on private capital, but the role of government in housing and mortgage markets will need to be defined before private markets will fully reengage. Any policy solution will have to be evaluated in the context of its effect on both owner-occupied and rental housing markets. And as the policy conversations progress, it will also be important to maintain a focus on the demand side of the market--which is to say, all of us, as consumers of housing. Finally, a national housing policy must also serve the needs of the segments of our society that have been historically underserved--low-income and low-wealth families, including disproportionate numbers of minorities and households headed by females.

These longer-term questions are critical. But before we get to the longer-term solutions, we need to deal with the unprecedented number of loans in or still entering the foreclosure pipeline, the disposition of properties acquired through foreclosure, and the effect of a high percentage of distressed sales on home prices. Regardless of how we got here, we, as a nation, currently have a housing market that is so severely out of balance that it is hampering our economic recovery.

To many, the story of the recent financial crisis and its aftereffects for the housing market is one mainly attributed to subprime lending. Although problems were concentrated initially in subprime mortgages, today about two-thirds of underwater mortgages and loans in foreclosure are actually prime or Federal Housing Administration (FHA) mortgages. This fact suggests that solutions aimed at righting the wrongs of previous reckless lending in the subprime market are not sufficient to tackle the scale of current problems.

Clearly, the market is not functioning as it should. Despite near-record-low interest rates, credit conditions remain tight for many consumers and investors interested in buying or refinancing residential real estate. Moreover, the lack of sufficient numbers of buyers and sellers may limit price discovery, which heightens uncertainty about the “right” price for a given piece of real estate and further limits activity. In addition, the large number of foreclosures and a protracted foreclosure process have led to an unprecedented level of bank-owned homes, a level that is likely to persist for some time.

So how do we move forward in these difficult circumstances? The economy normally has some self-correcting mechanisms. Typically, a drop in prices--whether the price of an apple or the price of a house--stimulates demand and brings new buyers into the market. In the case of houses, price declines often occur in the context of a broad-based weakness in the overall economy. In response to macroeconomic weakness, the Federal Reserve generally can lower the target federal funds rate, which would be expected to lower mortgage rates. The combination of lower prices and lower mortgage rates makes home purchase more affordable and helps revive the housing market. Indeed, most recent recoveries have been led by housing. But for a variety of reasons, these mechanisms are not working fully in today’s economy. When crafting solutions, it is helpful to first identify areas where removing some obstacles might enable these self-correcting mechanisms to operate more productively.

REFINANCING EXISTING MORTGAGES AT LOWER RATES

One way to reduce the flow of foreclosed homes is to ease the payment strain on borrowers, which can be accomplished by modifying loans that are past due or by refinancing performing loans at lower rates. The Federal Reserve has already acted to lower longer-term interest rates, including mortgage rates, through the purchase of longer-term Treasury securities, agency debt, and agency mortgage-backed securities. In addition to enabling more buyers to purchase homes, low mortgage rates act to reduce the debt service cost of existing household debt. However, while refinancing activity has picked up in response to the lower rates, the pickup has been subdued compared with past low-rate environments. That is, even though mortgage rates on many outstanding loans are well above current market rates, many borrowers have not been able to take advantage of the lower rates because they have little or no equity in their homes or face other obstacles.

To facilitate refinancing for borrowers who are current on their mortgages but whose equity has eroded as home prices have fallen, the Administration’s Home Affordable Refinance Program, or HARP, provides streamlined refinancing for low- or no-equity mortgages if the borrowers meet certain qualifications and if their existing mortgages are already guaranteed by Fannie Mae or Freddie Mac. So far, more than 800,000 borrowers have refinanced their mortgages through HARP.

One question, however, is why more borrowers have not benefited from this program. We estimate that 4 million borrowers appear to meet the basic eligibility for HARP refinancing.[1] Of course, some of these borrowers may be ineligible for reasons that we cannot observe, and others may be uninterested in refinancing. However, given the potential savings to households, the relatively low take-up on this program warrants another look at the frictions that may be impeding these refinancing transactions.

Responses to our inquiries regarding impediments to HARP refinancing have revealed four possible frictions:

1. *Loan-level pricing adjustments (LLPAs)*. LLPAs are upfront fees that are added to the refinancing costs of loans that are judged to have higher risk characteristics, such as high loan-to-value ratios. The fees can increase the cost of refinancing by thousands of dollars and thus discourage borrowers from participating in the HARP program. Risk-based pricing is a standard risk-management tool for lenders in evaluating new risk. However, when the lender or guarantor already owns the credit risk, refinancing a low- or no-equity loan can actually reduce risk because it reduces payments and thus makes default less likely.
2. *Limited lender competition for HARP refinance loans due to lender concerns about taking on "putback" risk from previous underwriting.* Putback risk is the possibility that the loan originator will have to repurchase the loan from the government-sponsored enterprises (GSEs) because the underwriting violated GSE guidelines. Although the streamlined HARP guidelines do not require lenders to verify all aspects of a borrower's application, lenders who process the HARP refinancings have putback risk both from the refinance and from the original underwriting, even if the refinancing lender did not underwrite the original loan. This risk may make lenders reluctant to refinance loans originated by other lenders and so limits participation in the program. Perhaps competition among potential lenders could be increased if a minimum number of timely payments could be used as a proxy for sound original underwriting to relieve the liability of the refinancing lender for the mistakes of previous lenders.

3. *Junior lienholders.* In some cases, holders of junior liens are refusing to allow their loans to remain subordinate to a proposed new refinance loan, thus holding up the HARP process.
4. *Mortgage insurers.* Similarly, some mortgage insurers will not agree to reunderwrite their policies despite presumably diminished default risk after the refinancing.

The common theme in all of these frictions is that, in each case, the parties to the transaction are applying standard risk-management tools that would normally apply to low- or no-equity loans--but they are applying them to risk they already own. The economics of the situation suggests that if the first mortgage becomes more affordable, the existing risk exposure of all credit risk holders actually decreases. Moreover, to the extent that more widespread refinancing reduces the overall volume of distressed mortgages, it likely reduces pressures on house prices which would, in turn, lead to lower losses on sales of foreclosed properties across all mortgage portfolios. And finally, removal of barriers to refinancing would boost the impetus to recovery provided by lower long-term interest rates. Thus, finding different approaches to the policies that are hindering refinancing would likely provide some support to the economic recovery while improving the circumstances of homeowners and reducing the overall level of credit risk borne by the various holders of the risk.

CONVERTING REAL ESTATE OWNED TO RENTAL

Let me turn now to the effect on the housing market of properties acquired by creditors through foreclosure, commonly called real estate owned, or REO. An estimated 1 million or more properties will likely pass through REO inventory in 2011, with another million or so per year expected in both 2012 and 2013.

REO properties are weighing heavily on the market for owner-occupied houses in at least three ways. First, REO properties increase the total inventory of properties for sale. While the numbers are difficult to measure precisely, we estimate that in the second quarter of 2011, roughly 500,000 to 600,000 of the 2 million vacant homes for sale in the United States were REO properties. This extra supply is particularly problematic because demand is quite low. High unemployment and tight credit standards are currently precluding many families from buying homes, and other potential buyers may be staying out of the market due to uncertainty about their incomes. Even ignoring the potential inventory represented by the large backlog of distressed loans that have not yet been foreclosed upon, the current inventory of existing homes for sale represents approximately nine months of sales compared with a norm of five to six months, suggesting additional pressure on house prices as the market struggles to clear the excess inventory. Second, the downward pressure on prices is compounded by the high proportion of sales considered to be distressed sales. Currently, around 40 percent of sales transactions are considered to be distressed sales--that is, short sales or sales of REO properties. And third, high vacancy rates and the low level of maintenance that often characterize foreclosed properties make a neighborhood a less desirable place to live and thus depress the value of surrounding homes.[2]

In contrast to the market for owner-occupied houses, the market for rental housing has been strengthening of late. For example, apartment rents have turned up in the past year, and vacancy rates on multifamily rental properties have dropped noticeably.

The relative strength of the rental market reflects increased demand as families who are unable or unwilling to purchase homes because of tight mortgage conditions or income uncertainty are renting properties instead. Rental demand has also been supported by families who have lost their homes to foreclosure. The majority of these families move to rental housing, most commonly to single-family rentals.[3] Unfortunately, these conditions supporting rental demand may persist for some time.

The weak demand in the owner-occupied housing market and the relatively high demand in the rental housing market suggest that transitioning some REO properties to rental housing might benefit both markets. Such conversions might also be in the best interests of lienholders and guarantors if recoveries from renting out properties exceed those from outright sales. Over time, as financing conditions ease and the number of REO properties to be sold declines, the share of properties sold to owner-occupants and sold to investors for rental will adjust commensurately.

Small investors are already converting some foreclosed properties to rental units on a limited scale. Larger-scale conversion, however, has been hindered by at least two factors. First, managing single-family rental homes is expensive unless the properties are concentrated within a geographic area and investors can be certain of acquiring a critical mass of properties. Second, regulatory guidance and standard servicing practices have typically encouraged GSEs, FHA, servicers, and financial institutions to actively market

REO properties for sale and to consider rentals only as a short-term income generator while the properties are being marketed.

In August, the Federal Housing Finance Agency (FHFA), working with the Treasury Department and the Department of Housing and Urban Development, issued a request for information seeking ideas for the disposition of REO owned by Fannie Mae, Freddie Mac, and the FHA, including ideas for turning these properties into rental housing. Together, the GSEs and the FHA hold about half of the outstanding REO inventory and so may be able to aggregate enough properties to facilitate a cost-effective rental program in many markets.

In thinking through how a rental program might be structured, I want to highlight three possible design considerations. First, as I noted earlier, achieving a cost-effective program may require obtaining a critical mass of properties--perhaps a couple hundred or more--within a limited geographic area. In this respect, the comparative advantage of government is in solving the aggregation problem.

The combined portfolios of the GSEs and the FHA are large enough to achieve the necessary scale in a number of markets. However, the structuring of such a program might require the flexibility for a pooling entity to acquire properties from more than one seller or to contract for the acquisition of a minimum number of properties over time. With such flexibility, the scale potential of the GSE-FHA portfolios could be supplemented with properties from servicer or financial institution portfolios.

Second, it is important to ensure that such rental conversions are executed in a responsible manner and in the best interests of renters and local communities. Replacing the blight of a foreclosed home with the blight of a rundown rental property would provide little assistance to the affected neighborhoods. Examining how best to ensure that landlords keep their properties well maintained will be crucial.

Third, in many markets, house prices have fallen to such an extent that better recoveries may result from renting properties rather than selling them. However, in other markets, converting REO properties to rentals may not be in the narrow best interest of financial institutions or mortgage investors but may be in the best interest of local communities. For these markets, it may be useful to consider the possible role of new incentives and, if so, what form those incentives might take.

While existing statutes and regulations do not prohibit financial institutions from renting REO properties, supervisors encourage sales as the primary disposition tool. In light of the relative weakness of the owner-occupied market and strength of the rental market along with the potential for a GSE-FHA program to solve the problem of insufficient scale in some markets, conditions are unusual enough that it might also make economic sense to clarify existing expectations to recognize that in some cases converting a portion of residential REO to rental may be a reasonable option for financial institutions. Depending upon the conditions in their individual markets, I believe having such an option could allow for better outcomes for institutions--that is, a superior net present value compared with traditional disposition approaches--and could at the same time contribute to market healing.

However, to be effective in promoting better outcomes, such an approach would require supervisors to clarify current supervisory guidance to address how existing standards might apply to the valuation of real estate converted to rental, the time limits applicable to such holdings, and other aspects of managing those properties. Financial institutions with large portfolios might be able to achieve scale in some markets on their own or possibly leverage the scale of a GSE-FHA program if such a program was created; smaller institutions should also have the flexibility to act in accordance with the conditions in their local markets.

Responsible REO Management

In addition to the consideration of conversion strategies at significant scale, there are steps that all REO holders can take today to ensure that they are not contributing further to the problems. They can and should make sure that they are adequately monitoring any third-party vendors with which they contract to maintain, market, or sell REO properties.

Certainly, the recent interagency review of servicers revealed the severe consequences that can result from failing to monitor third-party vendors. Before converting REO properties to rental, REO holders could also consider "first look" types of programs to enable owner-occupants, public entities, and nonprofits windows of time to bid on available properties. A number of institutions have used such programs with successful results. And REO holders who sell large numbers of properties to investors should consider processes, such as those used by the GSEs, to screen and monitor bulk investors to reasonably assess their probable actions regarding maintenance and disposition after acquiring the properties.

LOW-VALUE PROPERTIES

So far I've talked solely about REO-to-rental as a solution for REO properties. But that's not going to work everywhere. In particular, some properties are too damaged, or otherwise too low-value, to be sold as owner-occupied units or profitably converted to rental properties. In fact, we estimate that about 5 percent of properties in the REO inventory of the FHA and the GSEs are appraised at less than $20,000, and in some markets the share is significantly higher. In many of these cases, the cost to repair or demolish existing structures exceeds their fair market value, and a different type of solution may be needed. In recent years, local governments and community-based organizations have struggled to counter the effects of foreclosures on neighborhoods. One tool for controlling the temporary condition and ultimate disposition of REO properties is the use of a unique kind of entity known as a land bank.[4] Land banks are typically public or nonprofit entities created to manage properties not dealt with adequately through the private market. The lifespan of these entities may be time-limited with sunset provisions. The notion of a land *bank*, as opposed to a land *trust*, is that properties are brought in and moved out of a land bank's portfolio rather than permanently preserved. Using this kind of mechanism, a community can gain control of low-value properties that may otherwise sit vacant and cause problems for the surrounding neighborhood. Options available for disposing of the properties include physical rehabilitation, some period of rental, sale to new owner-occupants or responsible investors, or, in some cases, demolition. Because it likely will take several years for the overhang of vacant homes to be sold, such a strategy would help some communities deal with the short-term crisis and then ultimately allow for the disposition of properties in a manner suitable to local market conditions in the longer term. While few land banks currently have the resources to operate at significant scale, the land bank model is one that has shown some success and could help many communities stabilize troubled properties if used more extensively. However, although such an approach holds promise, the current infrastructure for land banks is limited.

CONCLUSION

These are my thoughts on some of the things that can be done in the near term to help the housing market stabilize and rebalance. An immediate priority is balancing supply and demand in a market overwhelmed by financially stressed homeowners, tight credit conditions, and an unusually high number of foreclosed homes. It is an important part of rebuilding our market for housing and housing finance, but it is only a part. In addition, we must think carefully about longer-term policy and market changes that may affect Americans' housing options for years and even decades to come. This is important work, and I appreciate your participation in the forum today.

Thank you.

End Notes

[1] This estimate is for borrowers who have mortgages guaranteed by Fannie Mae or Freddie Mac that were originated no earlier than 2003 and no later than May 31, 2009. The mortgages carry an interest rate on the first lien that is more than 75 basis points higher than the current level of mortgage rates and have loan-tovalue ratios on the first-lien mortgage that are between 80 and 125 percent. The borrowers are current on their loans and have missed either no payments in the past year if guaranteed by Freddie or a maximum of one payment in the past year if guaranteed by Fannie.

[2] See, for instance, John P. Harding, Eric Rosenblatt, and Vincent W. Yao (2009), "The Contagion Effect of Foreclosed Properties," *Journal of Urban Economics*, vol. 66 (November), pp. 164-78; and John Y. Campbell, Stefano Giglio, and Parag Pathak (2011), "Forced Sales and House Prices," *American Economic Review*, vol. 101 (August), pp. 2108-31.

[3] See Raven Molloy and Hui Shan (2011), "The Post-Foreclosure Experience of U.S. Households," Finance and Economics Discussion Series 2011-32 (Washington: Board of Governors of the Federal Reserve System, May), www.federalreserve.gov/Pubs/FEDS/2011/201132.

[4] For more information, see Thomas J. Fitzpatrick IV (2010), "How Modern Land Banking Can Be Used to Solve REO Acquisition Problems," in *REO and Vacant Properties: Strategies for Neighborhood Stabilization*, proceedings of the conference REO and Vacant Properties: Strategies for Neighborhood Stabilization cosponsored by the Federal Reserve Banks of Boston and Cleveland and the Federal Reserve Board, pp. 145-50, www.federalreserve.gov/events/conferences/2010/reovpsns/downloads/reo_20100901.pdf.First, not all states have passed legislation that is needed to permit land banks. Second, this is difficult work, and existing land banks have limited capacity to handle high numbers of properties at a time. More funding and technical assistance would be needed to scale these efforts up to an adequate level. Of course, new funds are hard to come by in the current fiscal environment, but this appears to be an instance where relatively modest investments have the potential to yield significant benefits, such as reduced crime stemming from vacant properties, lower municipal costs to limit property deterioration or provide services to neighborhoods that are largely vacant, higher property tax revenue derived from property values not being unduly depressed, and other benefits that may be realized.

INDEX

G

H

I

J

L

M